CHANGED BEHIND BARS
THE HISTORY OF MY REDEMPTION!
CHANDLER FOZARD

ISBN 13: 978-0-9824924-0-6

Cover and interior design by Bookcovers.com

AUTHOR'S INTRODUCTION

The church is full of hypocrites. I know this because I was one of them. I claimed to be a Christian while I used and abused everyone and everything around me. I did whatever I wanted, when I wanted, how I wanted, and I didn't care who I hurt in the process. I believed people existed for what they could give me and my thoughts and actions reflected that.

When I was 16 a pastor asked me to repeat a few words after him at the end of the service and—Presto! I was told I had said "the sinner's prayer" and had become a Christian. From that point on, I was in church every week, volunteered whenever I could, witnessed to others, preached, prayed, laid hands on the sick and had hands laid on me.

Attending church, even being active in church, didn't stop me from preying on others. I looked for those I could manipulate to get what I wanted and then I did, over and over again, victim after victim. Eventually I got caught and I was sent to more than one psychologist who attempted to help me learn how to control myself. I couldn't.

As I was becoming more and more aware of how wrong my desires were—not just before men but even before God since I was now in church, I began to intensify my efforts to find help. I tried everything my religion offered me: sheer will power, deliverance services—where a bunch of people laid hands on and tried to cast the devils out of me, even fasting and prayer. It seemed nothing or no one could save me. Then I was sentenced to 10 years in prison.

How is it that I, a professing Christian, ended up in prison? That was the question that plagued me from the time I was arrested until the night I begged God to have mercy on me. How did *I* end up in prison? I know the circumstances that surround people becoming Christians will be different. But I can tell you that I didn't become a Christian after I prayed with that pastor. How do I know that? How can I be certain I am even a Christian now? What made the prayer I prayed with the pastor different from the prayer I prayed in my cell?

People don't become Christians in a vacuum. Regardless of the circumstances, when someone becomes a Christian there is going to be some history behind it, even if it was just the last minute! The dictionary defines history as "a continuous, systematic narrative of past events...usually written as a chronological account."[1] And the Bible is often referred to as "the history of redemption." "Being saved" is about more than the moment I said that prayer. It stretches over the whole of my life, the whole of history, and even into eternity!

There are many books written about the way people become Christians from theological perspectives. And I have a few words to say about these in my "book blog" (see Appendix A) but I will leave the heavy lifting to those best suited. I am concerned with the events that made the decision to become a Christian real and not just another way to fix my problems. When and how did I really become a Christian? Again, what made the prayer I prayed in my prison cell differ from the prayer I prayed with the pastor?

According to Scripture, salvation is a lifelong process and that's why Paul wrote that "...the message of the cross is foolishness to those who *are perishing* but to us who *are being saved* it is

---

1   Source: Dictionary.com (http://dictionary.reference.com/browse/history)

the power of God." (I Corinthians 1:18, emphasis added.) The moment I finally stopped trying to fix myself and my problems and I turned to Christ—the moment I was converted, was a dramatic event but it was one of many. And without the historical context, I would never have been converted. I didn't become a Christian when I prayed with that pastor because, quite simply, it wasn't the right time. I hadn't learned enough about myself. I hadn't learned enough about Christ.

Some will accept Christ as the result of a series of almost imperceptible events. This is usually true for those who have been raised by Christian parents who taught them to believe that these things are just so. They have never strayed too far from the faith so as to require a "great awakening." They have been at the work of purifying their souls in obeying the truth for as long as they can remember. Timothy seems to be a Biblical example of these. God bless them!

There are others of us, however, whose lives have taken us to the depths of hell and back. We will often be able to pinpoint the moment we became Christians. We count among our numbers Rahab of old, the woman caught in adultery and another woman at a well. We had scarlet letters pinned to our chests and we wore them proudly! We know what it is to sin and, after we are truly converted, we know what it is to be saved by grace. As a result, we also know what it is to love our Savior in a way that some may never know (Luke 7:47).

Therefore, God is pleased to reveal Himself to some on a sunny day and others in the fierce, unthinkable storms of life. For this reason, it is not my intention to state that you're not a Christian if you're unable to recognize or don't believe you experienced a particular sequence of events prior to the time you believe you became a Christian. This isn't the 12 steps to become a Christian! (Somebody please shout, "Thank God!") It is not my intention to say that your experience must look like mine or that you must have felt as dramatically regarding your own conversion experience as did I.

This is the history of *my* redemption. It unfolds the horror of my sin, the grace of God, and the two are often side-by-side. The early chapters will focus on historical narratives from my life. Following each narrative, using Biblical hindsight, I will discuss where I believe I was on the road to redemption. In the later chapters, especially after I've become a Christian, the lessons I've learned from Scripture are intertwined with scenes from my life.

Chapters 1, 3, 5, and 7 are historical narratives

Chapters 2, 4, 6, and 8 discuss where I was on the road to redemption

Chapters 9 through 14 contain some narratives coupled with Biblical truths and discuss what I believe to be the most significant lessons I've learned since becoming a Christian.

Concluding, I will bring it all together with a summary of the stages of my salvation and, in view of those stages, a clear statement of the gospel that saves.

I am writing this book because I believe there are many who would accept Christ if they thought He could help—and He can. Don't let the hypocrites distract you. Don't let your own hypocrisy prevent you. No Christian is perfect. The only differences between Christians and those who haven't accepted Christ are that (1) we know we are screw ups (aka sinners), (2) we know we can't be good enough to please God, which is why (3) we have placed our faith and trust in Christ to save and transform us. This book is written to persuade you as best I know how that Christ will do much more than just "help" you; He'll change you. Forever!

Next, I am certain there are many who, as I once was, are "on the verge of total ruin, in the midst of the assembly and the congregation" (Proverbs 5:14). As Paul pleaded with his readers, so I plead with you, "Examine yourselves as to whether you are in the faith. Test yourselves..." (2 Corinthians 13:5). As you read the history of my redemption, I pray you'll—as some say today—"check yourself before you wreck yourself."

If you're like I was, you have a false sense of security because you believe you became a Christian when you said a few magic words or because of some good works you do. But have you really, finally trusted in Christ for your salvation? You may have an event but do you have the context; you may have an object of your faith but is it Christ?

Spurgeon said it better than I do: "Comparing ourselves among ourselves, we are not wise. I do believe there are hundreds and thousands who remain in doubt and darkness, and go down to despair. . . . Now, then, with all my might I come this morning to break down every barrier that keeps a soul from Christ; and, as God the Holy Spirit shall help me, to dash the battering ram of truth against every wall that has been built up, whether by doctrinal truth or experimental truth, that keeps the sinner from Christ, who desires to come and to be saved by him" (Excerpted from "Struggles of Conscience," September 22, 1860, http://www.biblebb.com/files/spurgeon/0336.htm).

Finally, I am writing to those trapped in the vilest of sins that have long ago lost hope. You've been to all the doctors. You have asked help of anyone who would listen and, if you were lucky, lend a hand. You've tried prescriptions, alcohol, illegal drugs, pornography, sexual activity, mayhem or maybe even murder. It seems nothing and no one can save you. Here is hope, real hope! Hope that won't disappoint you!

TABLE OF CONTENTS

CHAPTER ONE: SCHIZO

You'll soon read that both my parents are deceased and I was raised in group homes. There are so many questions left unanswered. I don't how they met, how they came to be here or there, and the same is true for much of my own history. Keep this in mind as you read. If you find yourself scratching your head and wondering what just happened, I'll just ask you to remember that (1) this isn't intended to be an autobiography and (2) the chances are pretty good that I just don't know.

Susan Anne Dickens, mom, was born to Patricia Dickens August 3, 1944. Patricia chose not to raise her, so "Susie" was adopted and raised by her grandparents, George and Hortense Dickens. As an adult, Susie married Paul McGill, with whom she had two children, Ryan and Nancy. They lived in Nebraska. Susie was unfaithful to Paul and that affair resulted in their divorce, her expecting another child and loss of the custody of her first two kids.

Susie answered an ad placed by a man named Stanley Fozard to be the caregiver for his son, Fergus. Soon after, she gave birth to the little girl, but Stanley made her give the baby away for adoption because he didn't think they could afford her. She continued to care for Fergus for a while and, somewhere along the way, she married Stanley. Susie was 28 and Stanley was 58.

On March 20, 1970, I was born—the only child to this couple in Kerrville, Texas. They named me Chandler David Fozard. Not long after, we moved to Carson City, Nevada.

The earliest memories I have of mom and dad are of them constantly fighting. I don't remember many "good times." I remember dad tending bar and always drinking Budweiser at home. I remember the loud fights, the throwing of objects, and one or the other of them storming out. I was too young to understand what was happening at the time. After dad moved to a town a hundred miles away "for a new job," I think they were on their way to a divorce, but that day never came.

Christmas Eve 1978, dad and his friend were on the way home for the holidays. Both men were drunk, but the other guy was driving and lost control of the car. Dad was killed instantly; the friend lived. Fergus and I were two curious kids listening from the cracked bedroom door when mom answered the knock from the highway patrolman. We heard him tell her that dad was dead. I think Fergus may have cried a little; I didn't shed a tear.

Christmas Day the same year, mom had a so-called nervous breakdown and became a textbook example of what secular psychologists would call a paranoid schizophrenic. We awoke to learn that dad wasn't really dead; he was alive and well and plotting to kidnap us with the help of "The Fozards." Mom began cursing out ceiling fans and carrying on conversations with people who weren't there. We would be driving from point A to point B and she would either begin following or trying to elude some other car that was supposed to be carrying "them"—the people who were trying to take us from her. One minute she would be in a daze, a woman on a mission to save her children; the next she would snap out of it and wouldn't have any idea where she was or why. Those were the good days.

On the bad days she would physically abuse Fergus. Later she would claim it was done out of resentment toward dad, who made her give up her baby girl while she still cared for Fergus.

In a moment of sanity, she decided to give Fergus away to an older half-brother from one of dad's earlier marriages. I never saw Fergus alive again.

From what I understand, Fergus began abusing drugs and constantly running away. I heard he began hopping trains as a form of transportation and was killed by one of them when he didn't make it. I may never know for sure. All I do know is I loved Fergus very much. The memories I have of him involve us playing with our dogs, being forced to watch "Marcus Welby, M.D.," and Lawrence Welk, or getting our bare butts whipped by mom for something we had done, lying and crying together, side-by-side on the bed. The fondest memories I have, however, are of him saving my life, not once, but twice!

Growing up I was a pretty sick kid. I was in and out of hospitals with severe allergic reactions all the time. I also had childhood epilepsy, complete with grand-mal seizures. During one such seizure, I began to swallow my tongue. Fergus used a spoon to hold it in place while my seizure continued, using the phone to call for help with his other hand. Watching all those episodes of "Marcus Welby, M.D." paid off!

Another time we were at the weekly motel where dad was living while at his new job. I was edging around the deep end of the pool and slipped. Fergus, who was a strong swimmer, pulled me back to the edge. After mom gave Fergus away, I wasn't sure how I was going to manage to live the rest of life without him being there to save me!

Now it was just mom and me. I think she managed to live off of Social Security and welfare because I don't really remember her working much. She did work as a home health aide a couple of times, but that's all I can remember. I don't imagine being a "paranoid schizophrenic" lent itself very well to regular employment. Eventually, we moved to Dallas, Texas, where mom was convinced "the grass was greener." She called it "the savior state" because Texas would be where everything got better . . . or not.

It wasn't long before the public school in Texas began to notice that we had some serious issues. There was something really wrong with a mother who would show up at the school demanding to know why and where they let The Fozards take her son and a son who told the same story when confronted, even embellishing the tale. The school convinced her to take me for a psychological evaluation.

I was placed in Cliff House, an in-patient, mental diagnostic facility, for a couple of months of observation. At my request, mom picked me up and took me home before the evaluation was complete. They convinced her to take me in for outpatient examinations. Dr. John Keggrreis recommended immediate hospitalization and I became a patient at Terrel State Hospital, Terrel, Texas. That was August 11, 1981. I would be in ten different residential treatment facilities before I turned eighteen.

Some people live their whole lives with the worst of their sin hidden in their hearts and minds. Not me. By the age of eleven, I was a spanking fetishist. I derived sinful pleasure from the spanking of males. I would prey on guys who could never seem to get their act together. We would agree on the rules and I would spank them whenever they got into "trouble" by breaking the "rules." I would justify my perversion by telling myself I was really "helping" them. Perhaps that's how they justified it also.

By God's preserving grace, I never went beyond spanking. I experimented with homosexuality a couple of times when I was a teenager but that held little appeal for me. I was almost asexual. I wasn't attracted to guys for anything other than spanking, and I wasn't attracted to females at all. Although I wasn't a "child molester" in the way that most people use it, I was a predator in every sense of the word.

> *"The disease of self runs through my blood*
> *It's a cancer, fatal to my soul."*
> *Excerpted from In the Light by DC Talk*

CHAPTER TWO: BORN IN SIN

"Behold, I was brought forth in iniquity,
And in sin my mother conceived me." (Psalm 51:5)

I was born a sinner. This is referred to as the doctrine of original sin. Adam and Eve sinned and I inherited a sinful nature as a consequence of that sin (Genesis 3:15; Romans 5:12). It's not merely that I was born *into* a sinful world or born *influenced by* sin. It's that I was born with a nature enslaved to sin. It is not that sin is in my flesh, as if the flesh itself is somehow evil, but it is that my heart is hell-bent.

The Bible states that I went astray right out of the womb, that I came forth speaking lies, and that the thoughts and inclinations of my heart are only evil continually (cf. Gen 6:5, 8:21; Psalm 51:5, 58:3; Matt 15:19).[2] In *Confessions*, Augustine wrote that we can know this is true because we can see it in the actions of infants as they cry incessantly, demanding what they want, or in toddlers as they fight over some toy.

I don't remember what I was like as an infant. My memories are too faint to even describe what I may have been like as a toddler or even a young boy. Now middle-aged, I have perpetrated, experienced, and witnessed what theologians call the "total depravity of man"—my own in particular. I believe that,

---

2   Chapter Disclaimer: When I refer to being born in and under the power of sin and having a sinful nature in this Chapter, I am referring to my nature *apart from Christ*. After Christ, I am given a new nature. Although the war still rages, which we will address in a different chapter, there is a distinct difference between the nature and reign of sin in my life prior to becoming a Christian. There must be; else Christ died in vain.

apart from Christ, sin has corrupted and enslaved every part of my faculty, and this includes my will. I know my will is enslaved to sin because I have a sinful heart.

> *"The heart is deceitful above all things,*
> *And desperately wicked;*
> *Who can know it?" (Jeremiah 17:9)*

Since my heart is wicked, then everything I believe is wicked.

> *"The lamp of the body is the eye. If therefore your eye is good,*
> *your whole body will be full of light. But if your eye is bad,*
> *your whole body will be full of darkness. If therefore*
> *the light that is in you is darkness, how great is that darkness!"*
> *(Matthew 6:22,23)*

What Christ is saying in the above passage is that, if the presuppositions around which I orient my life are wrong, I will orient my whole life around whatever I believe. If a choice comes between doing what's right or what pleases me, I will choose the pleasure of sin because that's what I believe is most important. (The good news is that the reverse is true also!)

> *"No one can serve two masters; for either he will hate*
> *the one and love the other, or else he will be loyal*
> *to the one and despise the other. You cannot serve*
> *God and mammon." (Matthew 6:24)*

So everything begins in the heart. **If my heart is wicked, then everything I think, say, and do will be wicked.**

> *"For as he thinks in his heart, so is he." (Proverbs 23:7)*

> *"For out of the heart proceed evil thoughts,*
> *murders, adulteries, fornications, thefts, false*
> *witness, blasphemies. These are the things*
> *which defile a man. . ." (Matthew 15:19,20)*

In my case, my greatest desire was to be in control of and spank guys. So I was constantly on the prowl for relationships that would allow me to do just that. Moving all of the time taught me that relationships didn't matter because they didn't last. I learned how to use and abuse everyone and everything around me. People existed for what they could give me. They were objects, means to my own ends. If you had something to offer, I could be quite charming. If you had nothing, I would have a hard time even remembering your name.

If someone had accused me of having such a worldview when I was eleven, I would have said they were crazy. I never woke up and consciously decided I was going to be evil. I just was. A whale swims in the ocean. No one makes it swim, it just does. Swimming is its nature. Sinning was my nature. Pick your poison; spanking was mine.

And so I moved from group home to group home, acting according to my nature.

> "As it is written: 'There is no one righteous, not even one;
> there is no one who understands, no one who seeks God.
> All have turned away, they have together become worthless;
> there is no one who does good, not even one.'" (Romans 3:10-12)

Explain and defend your answers from Scripture and, when possible, from your own experience.

1. Do you believe you were born in sin?

   _____

   _____

   _____

2. What does it mean to be "born in sin"?

   _____

   _____

   _____

3. Do you believe that, apart from Christ, your heart is wicked?

_____

_____

_____

4. Do you believe that what's in your heart—what you believe about you and the world around you, what you feel is most important, determines the way you live?

_____

_____

_____

5. Apart from Christ, is there *anything* good in one who is born in sin?

_____

_____

_____

NOTES

_____

_____

_____

_____

_____

_____

CHAPTER THREE: A TEENAGE PREDATOR

The state didn't know what to do with me. Initially, I think most were convinced it was just a phase. Charging, prosecuting and sentencing me would be difficult because I was still a kid and my sin involved others my own age. Left unchecked, however, many thought that it could lead to more heinous acts. And as incident upon incident began to pile up, my caseworker became concerned and sought "help."

The first psychologist introduced me to "masturbatory desensitization"—no, I am not kidding. The idea was that I would begin to masturbate to my fantasy and then replace it just before ejaculation with the worst scenario imaginable. There was just one problem: I didn't know how to masturbate. The doctor used his hands in the air to give me a demonstration of how one might begin to do so. In so doing, of course, he introduced me to yet another pattern of sin to which I became enslaved.

The next "doctor" thought the first therapist was just plain nuts, no doubt believing himself to be more enlightened. Everyone knows a leopard can't change his spots (Jeremiah 13:23). Homosexuals can't change. Pedophiles won't stop molesting. Alcoholics or drug addicts are never cured; they are forever in "recovery." No matter how much I told him I wanted to change, he said I couldn't; my only hope was to find someone with whom I could act out my fantasies in the context of a relationship. "Or," he added, "If you don't, you'll be in prison before you're 25."

*****

One of the facilities I was in along the way was run by a group of wealthy ladies who organized as the Society for Abandoned and Neglected Children, known as SANCI. The previous facilities in which I was placed had somewhere between 45 and 500 kids on campus, some co-ed, some not. SANCI was different. The ladies wanted it to be as close to a family setting as possible. So, although the home was licensed for something like eight to ten kids, we seldom had more than six.

I saw two sets of house parents come and go. Both were no doubt Christians. The first set may well have left as a result of my sin. I may never know. It was this couple, however, who were persistent in their efforts to win me to Christ. I had little interest in going to their church. I was a teenager and wanted to do things my own way. After weeks of their persistence, however, I finally gave in and went to a Sunday morning service.

I have no idea what the sermon was about that morning. At the end of the service, I went forward to meet the pastor. He looked me in the eye and said, "Look, I know you're in a foster home. I know that because your foster parents asked me to pray with them last week because they were awaiting some new kids. Son, I am not going to begin to tell you that I know how you're feeling or what it's like being you. As far as I know, my parents came off the ark as pastors. What I do know is this: God is a father to the fatherless and Jesus wants to be your best friend, and I suspect you need each right about now. If you'll pray this prayer with me, Christ will become your best friend and He'll never leave you nor forsake you." So I did.

Later, with a gleam in their eye, my foster parents told me that I had prayed the sinner's prayer and accepted Christ. As for me, I was convinced I'd become a Christian. I destroyed my rock music, threw myself into the theology, witnessed, laid hands on the sick, and saw what I believed to be genuine miracles. I dressed as Jesus on Halloween, and I led teen after teen to destroy his or her heavy metal albums and "follow Christ" with me. I went to the church's summer camp, was "baptized in the Holy Spirit with the evidence of speaking in tongues," and even won the trophy for "Best Boy Worshipper"!

Between the ages of 11 and 18, I was in ten different facilities. One of the ten was an emergency shelter where each stay was supposed to be limited to 30 days at a time. I was there once for more than 60 days, and I was there a total of ten times between placements!

At 18, I aged out of the system. The next several years are a blur. I attended Job Corps in Roswell, New Mexico. Disappointed with the curriculum, I left Job Corps and made Roswell my home for a while. Eventually, I was hired and trained to sell Medicare supplementary policies by one of the best insurance sales trainers in the nation. When the federal government stepped in and decided to regulate Medicare supplements, and our commissions, I left the business. With the help of an investor, I bought a distributorship that sold gold-plated chains by the inch. That venture ended almost as fast as it began. Failure after failure piled up until I somehow found myself selling water filtration systems.

I was 21 with the words of the second psychologist ringing in my ears—"You need to find a way to act out your fantasies in the context of a relationship or you will be in prison before you're 25"—when I met a lady with three children.

Why is it that I always have to learn the hard way?

Some people gotta learn the hard way
I guess I'm the kinda guy
That has to find out for myself...

I thought the devil was a friend of mine
I turned my back on everything that was true
And wasted years that belong to you...

Left to myself, I realize
I am the maker of my own demise

The warning signs are like flares in the night
Still I proceed my greed is in spite of the fire
I know that's bound to burn

Why is it that I always gotta learn...
The hard way.

Excerpted from *The Hard Way* by D.C. Talk

NOTES

_____

_____

_____

_____

_____

_____

_____

_____

_____

_____

_____

_____

_____

_____

_____

_____

CHAPTER FOUR:
THE SCHOOL OF HARD KNOCKS

It's obvious when I say that I've been to "the school of hard knocks," what I mean is that I've learned some or all of what I know the hard way. In Biblical terms, being under the law is the equivalent of going to the school of hard knocks. According to Scripture, the purpose of the law is to convict me of sin and to teach me that I cannot save myself. Unfortunately, I am a slow learner.

I knew I had a problem. I knew what I was doing was wrong. What I didn't know was what to do about it or how to solve it. The state's answer was to send me to their psychologists. The first doctor wanted me to exchange one sin for another. The second wanted me to throw in the towel and embrace sin with vigor, so long as I found a way to do what I wanted legally.

But secular psychology can never produce the kind of change that pleases God. For "How can Satan cast out Satan?" (Mark 3:23). Its humanistic philosophy is fundamentally opposed to God because it teaches that I have everything I need within to solve my problems—albeit not without the costly and sometimes never-ending help from the so-called professionals and their drugs!

I recognized that what the psychologists wanted me to do was inconsistent with my newfound "faith"—even if I was still in my sin.

I knew the Scripture spoke against lust and unnatural desires. If the state couldn't solve my problem, that meant it was up to me. Not unlike Sarai offering Hagar to Abraham, I began to look for an answer to my problems on my own (Genesis 16:1-6).

When the pastor asked me to pray the sinner's prayer, it seemed the natural thing to do. Surely God could fix me. For me, praying that prayer was the same as if I had just applied for and been accepted into the school of hard knocks!

According to Scripture, the law is written on my heart so that I should instinctively know right from wrong:

> *". . . for when Gentiles, who do not have the law,*
> *by nature do the things in the law, these, although*
> *not having the law, are a law to themselves,*
> *who show the work of the law written in their hearts,*
> *their conscience also bearing witness, and between*
> *themselves their thoughts accusing or else*
> *excusing them." (Romans 2:14, 15)*

But it is also written that it is part of my nature to suppress that truth, to exchange it for a lie, and to worship the creation instead of the Creator:

> *"For the wrath of God is revealed from heaven against all*
> *ungodliness and unrighteousness of men, who suppress the*
> *truth in unrighteousness...who exchanged the truth of God*
> *for the lie, and worshipped and served the creature*
> *rather than the Creator. . . ." (Romans 1:18, 25)*

For, although I was born with a sense of right and wrong, sin had so marred my recognition of the truth that I wouldn't recognize it even when it was staring me in the face!

> *". . . I would not have known covetousness unless the*
> *law had said, 'You shall not covet. But sin, taking*
> *opportunity by the commandment, produced in me*
> *all manner of evil desire. For apart from the law, sin was dead.*
> *I was alive once without the law, but when the*

*commandment came, sin revived and I died. And the
commandment, which was to bring life, I found
to bring death. For sin, taking occasion by the commandment,
deceived me, and by it killed me." (Romans 7:7-11)*

But, since the law is holy and good, how does sin use it to kill me? That a commandment is given leads me to believe that (1) I am able to obey it on my own and that (2) I will save myself by doing so. But sin deceives me for I cannot obey the law on my own (Romans 8:7). And since the same law requires the death of the sinner, sin uses the very commandments that are to bring me life (were it not for my sinful nature) to result in my death. This death takes place in two ways. The first death takes place spiritually when sin separates me from God; the second death is literal and occurs when I die.

So when Paul wrote that sin killed him, he meant it; "For the wages of sin is death. . . " (Romans 6:23). But you've also heard the expression "It kills me." It is often used to express the frustration someone feels when he or she sees him- or herself unable to change something, someone, or the circumstances of life. I am sure we've all said, "I don't get it; it just kills me." I think that's also part of what Paul is describing here: the exasperation and helplessness I feel when I learn that I am a sinner and that I am unable to change no matter what I do. Yet, even this first death is a process: the law must continually show me my inability to satisfy its requirements until, finally, it kills me and I admit my powerlessness and inability to save myself. For me, it would be a slow, agonizing death!

Knowing what the law requires, knowing right from wrong, I continually fail to measure up. The more I learn, the more I am aware of my inability to please God. This cycle of frustration defeats and "kills me." Apart from Christ's intervention, despairing of my inability to save myself, I am left in a despair that can only lead to death. Again, however, the purpose of the law is to convict me of my sin. Even after I've come to Christ the law stands as a reminder of my inability to please God. But the law itself will never save me.

Prior to that altar call, sin had been unchecked by even the law of God in my heart. For no one had taken the time to introduce me to its author. After I said that prayer, I began to see what I was doing as sin. It wasn't just a personal problem now. I was a sinner in the hands of an angry God!

Before the law came, I had a vague recognition of sin, but sin was alive and well; after the law came, I now knew that it was God who judged my sin, and sin became exceedingly sinful. It wasn't just me feeling bad about what I was doing. The God of the universe was saying, "No," but the fruit still looked satisfying, pleasant to my eyes, and able to give me power in at least one area of my life (Genesis 3:6; Matthew 4:3, 6 and 9; I John 2:16). The awareness that I am disobeying God's law isn't enough to change me, however, for I am still carnal and "sold under sin" (Romans 7:14). This says something about the effect of my sinful nature: neither the threat of prison nor even death, whether spiritually or literally speaking, was enough to change me. It has been said, "You can't legislate morality," and this is why.

Many Christians would say, "Just quit. You can do it. Just give it to Christ." The problem was that I couldn't quit. I was as powerless over sin after saying that prayer as I'd been before. The only real difference was that I now knew I was a sinner. God's wrath abided on me and I was powerless to change. Like the sinner, almost-converted person, described in Romans 7:18 and following:

> *"For I know that in me (that is, in my flesh) nothing good dwells; for to will is present with me, but how to perform what is good I do not find. For the good that I will to do, I do not do; but the evil I will not to do, that I practice. Now if I do what I will not to do, it is no longer I who do it, but sin that dwells in me. I find then a law, that evil is present with me, the one who wills to do good. For I delight in the law of God according to the inward man. But I see another law in my members, warring against the law of my mind, and bringing me into captivity to the law of sin which is in my members."(Romans 7:18-23)*

It's not that I didn't want to stop sinning. Of course I wanted to stop sinning! Walk up and ask any alcoholic if he or she thinks he or she should stop drinking, any drug addict if she should stop taking drugs, any pedophile if he wants to stop molesting children. I am sure you can find a few who are so blinded by sin they see nothing wrong with it. They may well have been turned over to their own sinful desires, never to return (Romans 1:24). But this isn't the typical response! If asked, the most habitual sinners will surely agree that the law is good (Romans 7:16); they will agree that it would be great if they could change. They will agree with the Scriptures you quote that say they should change, that it's not God's will for them to continue in sin. I certainly did!

You have no idea the nights I spent crying out to God to be free. The cynic will say I was just crying over the consequences of my sin, and there's truth to that, but that wasn't all the truth. I tell you I was in pain, real pain, and I was dying in my sins! The good news of the gospel is that, just as Christ wept at the tomb of Lazarus over the unbelief of those closest to Him, Christ was weeping over me! He doesn't take pleasure in the death of the wicked. Thank God He didn't take pleasure in the death of this wicked one! Thank you God that you saw my pain, wept over me . . . and provided the way of salvation for me!

"O wretched man that I am! Who will deliver me from this body of death? I thank God—through Jesus Christ our Lord!"
(Romans 7:24, 25)

In Romans 1 through 3, Paul details the evil that all men do when we exchange the truth of God for a lie. Every so-called professional I consulted, all the hands I allowed to be laid on me in the context of so-called deliverance services, every vain prayer and fast, these were all attempts to save myself. It didn't matter that I was in church. Like the adulterer described by the writer of Proverbs:

"I was on the verge of total ruin, In the midst of the assembly, and the congregation." (Proverbs 5:14)

I can tell you with a certainty that, if I'd died then, I would have been one of those the Lord would not have known. Although I spoke in the tongues of men and angels, I continued to practice sin. From all outward appearances, I had a form of godliness, but inwardly I denied its real power: the power to turn from sin (2 Timothy 3:5). I shudder when I venture to think about how many others are lost in our churches! What about you? Are you in the church while still dead in your sin? I was one of those to whom Christ was referring when He said:

"Not everyone who says to Me, 'Lord, Lord,' shall enter the kingdom of heaven, but he who does the will of My Father in heaven. Many will say to Me in that day, 'Lord, Lord, have we not prophesied in Your name, cast out demons in Your name, and done many wonders in Your name?' And then I will declare to them, 'I never knew you; depart from Me, you who practice lawlessness!'" (Matthew 7:21-23)

But what contributed to my sin? What poured gas on the fire? What resulted in so much unnecessary hurt and pain in my life and the lives of those against whom I sinned? It is the common denominator found in all false gospels: the idea that I could save myself. The true gospel declares that I am a sinner, justly deserving of the wrath of God and without hope, unless God in His sovereign mercy saves me through Jesus Christ. Anything that adds to or takes away from any part of that truth is a false gospel.

Any attempt by me to save myself, to solve my problems on my own, apart from Christ, only results in greater sin, pain and misery for both me and those affected by my sin. Any attempt by others to help me save myself, to help me solve my problems apart from Christ, to increase my "self-esteem" or to motivate me to change with encouraging pep talks, actually deprives me of the real medicine I need to cure the fatal disease of sin. It's not loving, it's not merci-ful, to excuse sin or to try to remedy sin through any other means than the true gospel. It's just evil. And God told Jer-emiah to tell the people how angry He was because they would continually try to save themselves, using their own means, instead of the means He has provided for their salvation:

"For My people have committed two evils: They have forsaken Me, the fountain of living waters, and hewn themselves cisterns—broken cisterns that can hold no water."
(Jeremiah 2:13)

Secular psychology, the message of that pastor, deliverance services, **all of these were "broken cisterns that can hold no water"—they all promise refreshment, but there was no water from the Word to cleanse.** I sought counsel from the so-called experts, asked advice from just about anyone who would listen, but it seemed that nothing and no one could save me. As is said regarding the woman with female problems that seemed they would never end:

"And there was a woman who had had a discharge of blood for twelve years, and though she spent all her living on physicians, she could not be healed by anyone." (Luke 8:44)

It seemed nothing or no one could save me. If only I'd known who it was who offered me a drink, I would never have thirsted again! (John 4:10). But the Scripture teaches that the thoughts and intents of my heart are desperately wicked. I must have a new heart and truth outside of myself if I am to be changed (Jeremiah 17:9; John 3:5).

It has been said that sin will take you further than you ever intended to go and it will keep you longer than you ever intended to stay. That was certainly true for me and it wasn't long before I was going further on the downward spiral of sin than I ever would have believed possible. I had found the perfect pretext for my sin: I would be a step-dad!

"There is a way that seems right to a man,
But its end is the way of death." (Proverbs 14:12)

1. Now that you have learned that your conscience is really the law of God, are you able to look back and see the times that God was calling to you, pleading with you not to sin? To turn to Him?

   _____

   _____

   _____

2. Give some examples of ways in which you've suppressed and exchanged the truth of God for lies.

   _____

   _____

   _____

3. Do you see ways in which, past or present, you have worshipped the creation instead of its Creator?

   _____

   _____

   _____

4. What does Paul mean by the law "killed him" (Romans 7:13)? How so?

   _____

   _____

   _____

5. There is a longstanding debate regarding Romans 7:14-25. The majority position believes Paul is describing the everyday struggle a Christian faces with indwelling sin; those in the minority, among which is the author, hold that Paul is describing the life of one just before he becomes a Chris-

tian. Those who believe the former will point out that the person in the text is said to delight in God according to the inward man and that it's not possible for a sinner to delight in the law, since sin wars against God (Romans 8:7); those who believe the latter point out that the passage clearly states that (1) the man is still in his sin (v. 14), and (2) he is still *practicing* sin. Those in the minority position certainly believe that the Scripture teaches that the Christian still wrestles with sin, but they just don't believe *this* passage is describing that struggle. Where do you stand? What does your Christian walk tell you? If you believe this passage is describing a Christian, how would you defend your position against the other side? Likewise, if you believe it is not describing a Christian, defend your position also.

_____

_____

_____

6. The author states there is a sense in which every sinner delights in the law, agreeing with the law that it would be great if he or she didn't sin. Do you agree or disagree?

_____

_____

_____

7. Compare and contrast the temptations found in Genesis 3:6, Matthew 4:3, 6, 9, and in I John 2:16 with your own temptations. How should this understanding help you?

_____

_____

_____

8. Do you confess that, apart from Christ, you are a sinner, justly deserving of the wrath of God and powerless to save yourself?

_____

_____

_____

9. What did God want us to learn from Jeremiah's question, "Can a leopard change its spots?" (Jeremiah 13:23)

_____

_____

_____

10. What is the gospel?

_____

_____

_____

11. What is the common denominator among all false gospels?

_____

_____

_____

12. Like the woman with the issue, apart from Christ, how many "cures" have you sought? Which one, if any, has brought you freedom?

_____

_____

_____

13. What does the Scripture mean when it says that the children of Israel have exchanged "fountains of living water" for "broken cisterns that can hold no water"?

_____

_____

_____

14. Can you give an example of how you have done this?

_____

_____

_____

15. What good have they really done for you?

_____

_____

_____

16. From whence does the only water that can cleanse come?

_____

_____

_____

17. Were you in church before you came to prison?

_____

_____

_____

18. Did you profess Christ before you came to prison?

_____

_____

_____

19. What is the "power of godliness"? (2 Timothy 3:5)

_____

_____

_____

NOTES

_____

_____

_____

_____

_____

_____

_____

_____

_____

_____

_____

CHAPTER FIVE: THE END OF MY WAY

I was on a sales call in Antlers, Oklahoma, selling water filtration units to homeowners. I came to the place in my presentation at which I was supposed to make a comment about having a wife. Not being married at that time, I changed it up and said, "Well, this is the part where I am supposed to tell you that I have a wife who tells me how much money she spends on cleaning supplies, but I guess I can't say that because I'm not married yet" and I kind of laughed at the end when I said it.

The well-intentioned older couple looked at me with gleams in their eyes and said, "Well, you want to get married? You should meet our daughter!" They went on to tell me she was a young widower with three children: a 12-year-old boy, a 10-year-old boy, and a 7-year-old girl. And I was thinking, I confess now, not one but three kids to spank.

The lady and her children and I became an instant hit. The ground rules were laid: I would handle all the discipline and spanking would be the primary form of punishment. What I couldn't account for was the effect their relationship would have on me. **Until then, most people were just objects to me—means to my own ends.** This mom trusted me. Her kids loved me. With a conscience alive, sin became exceedingly sinful.

I confessed to my pastor at the time what I was feeling. I asked him, "Is it possible that God is using this to change me into the man He wants me to be?" And he answered, "Yes, Chandler. It's possible. But, if you want my support in this relationship, we need to tell the mom everything." So we did.

My pastor and I sat down and explained everything to her. After listening, she simply replied, "Well, you've been fighting this too long on your own. We'll get through this together." Astonished, to teary-eyed me, the pastor said, "Well, Chandler, it looks like you've found someone really special."

I am not going to say that I never spanked the kids again. I did. What I can say with certainty is that the thoughts and intent of my heart were different. Prior to that day, I would spank at every given opportunity. After that day, I began to look for other ways to discipline. I was pursuing my fiancé romantically and becoming a father the kids loved.

Around the same time, my mother inherited some money from her dad. Relatives she hadn't heard from or seen in years came out of the woodwork. Everyone wanted a piece. I pleaded with her to hire a trustee and not to let the newfound relatives manage it. On more than one occasion, I exchanged words with them. Although none of them had spoken with me in decades, with their only motivation being that they wanted me out of the picture, one of them made a call to the Department of Human Services and accused me of child molestation.

Unknown to my fiancé or to me, the kids were immediately pulled out of school and questioned. Friends, family, and educators were interviewed. In the end, we were told that not one word of testimony from anyone substantiated any of the claims made against me.

The caseworker began, "Mr. Fozard, you'll be glad to know that we have investigated what was said about you. We find no reason why anyone should say such things. Everyone with whom we have spoken says you're the best thing that's ever happened to those kids. The kids love you."

Then she asked, "So that we can close this case and let you get on with your lives, could you tell us the names of three references we could call who will say you'd be a good dad? And can you think of any reason why anyone would say these things against you? Is there anything else we need to know?"

And that's when I did the unthinkable: I confessed. I gave her my whole history, even the name of my caseworker from when I was in group homes. I begged for her help. Not long after, I was arrested; the DA used bad checks I'd written to have me charged with "Uttering Two or More Bogus Checks Exceeding $50" while they built a case against me for child abuse.

Among other charges, I went to court facing three counts of "Injury to a Minor Child," each carrying up to life in prison. My court-appointed attorney argued successfully that the children I abused had none of the injuries envisioned under that statute. The judge amended the charge to Caretaker Abuse, which carried up to ten years in prison. In the fall of 1992, I pled out to three, ten-year sentences to run concurrently and one five-year, suspended sentence with probation.

***

I arrived at the Lexington Assessment and Reception Center (Lexington, OK) in December 1992. Although I knew I had committed many sins worthy of my sentence and more, I still believed I was innocent of the charges in the specific case against me. After all, hadn't the pastor agreed with me? Wasn't I really beginning to get better? Hadn't all those people said I was a great dad? Didn't the kids love me? I could not help but feel I'd been wrongly imprisoned. "But God, I don't understand! For once in my life I seemed to be doing things right and You still let me end up here. Why?" That's when I read about Abraham and Abimlech.

In Genesis 20, Abraham was afraid that someone might try to kill him to get to his wife, Sarah. Abraham decided to tell anyone who asked that she was his sister. Evidently, Sarah's beauty and Abraham's lie had come to the attention of King Abimelech, for the king promptly took Sarah into his harem. But God intervened in a dream before the king touched her. God told the king he was a dead man for taking another man's wife. Abimelech pled with God regarding his innocence because (1) he hadn't touched her yet and (2) Abraham had lied to him. God agreed with the king but then He added, "Yes, I know that you did this in the integrity of your heart. For I also withheld you from sinning against Me; therefore I did not let you touch her" (Genesis 20:6).

After reading the account in Genesis 20, I came to believe that God must have restrained me from sinning, just as He had the king, for the protection of those against whom I sinned. **I was evaluating my innocence or guilt solely on the basis of the technicalities of man-made laws, but God knew the thoughts and intent of my heart (Matthew 5:27, 28). Not only was I guilty, but I tremble to think about how far I may have gone without His restraint.**

But surely I didn't deserve ten years! After all, I wasn't that bad of guy. In *The Institutes of the Christian Religion*, John Calvin wrote that my eyes often seem adequate when I am looking at the world and others around me. If for a moment on a sunny day, however, I turn my eyes toward heaven and attempt to gaze into the sun, I must quickly shield my eyes from its brightness. It is the same way with regard to my sin and the holiness of God. If I merely compare myself to another, it is easy to think of myself as not as bad as someone else. But when I came face to face with God's holiness, I am confronted with the depth of my own depravity and I am left with nothing to say.

Still believing myself to be a Christian—albeit an unsuccessful one—I began to intensify my efforts to cleanse myself of sin. The last broken pot I would use to try to save myself was fasting and prayer because, after all, "this kind comes out only prayer and fasting" (Matthew 17:21). Somewhere along the way, I told an inmate of my desire to write a book about how I'd been set free from sin through fasting and prayer. He suggested I write Mount Zion Bible Church, Pensacola, Florida, a ministry which, among other treasures, had its own press. (Of course, I hadn't been set free from sin yet, but no one needed to know that! It would happen.)

Michael Shelton responded to my inquiry. Sure they'd help! While I was writing, he suggested, I might want to read some literature he would send me. When I think about what I was proposing to write, his answer still amazes me! He could have responded that I was a sinner who had much to learn. He could have proceeded to intellectually shred me. He didn't. He simply accepted me where I was, offered assistance, and then inundated me with the gospel.

The mission of this ministry, and it would seem the message of all of the authors they would freely send me, is "to humble the pride of man, to exalt the grace of God in salvation, and to promote real holiness in heart and in life." All of the authors whose works they sent emphasized the depravity of man and the sovereignty of God in salvation.

The literature they sent would be the end of me trying to do everything my way. In God's providence, I would learn about a grace that was greater than my sin. But before that could happen, I desperately needed to learn how desperately wicked I am without Him.

NOTES

_____

_____

_____

_____

_____

_____

CHAPTER SIX: TOTAL DEPRAVITY

E arlier I wrote that I was born in sin, but the doctrine of total depravity teaches more than just that we are born in sin.

Total depravity does not mean that I am as bad as I can be or that I never do anything good. It means that sin has enslaved every part of my faculty, including my will. I don't remember the first author I read who mentioned that I was totally depraved, powerless over and enslaved to sin. I remember my reaction the first time I read it: "Duh!" I thought to myself. Of course I am powerless over my sin! At last! Someone finally agrees that I really am messed up and that it is going to take more than my own willpower to change me. Still, I couldn't deny that this whole emphasis on my depravity and powerlessness seemed like such a novel concept!

Before my incarceration, I had belonged to some of the largest churches in Texas. These churches emphasized "the authority of the believer" and the God-like abilities that we are supposed to have once we become Christians. They raised the most money, had the largest budgets, employed the highest-paid pastors, and had the largest orchestra pits, the best praise bands, and the most famous teachers. They owned the largest television stations and held the largest crusades. How could so many be wrong? I look back now and remember a line I saw in an old film produced by Concordia about Martin Luther. In that film, Luther asked, "Is all the world blind and I alone condemned to see?" I have no idea whether that's an actual quote, but I can tell you it accurately described how I felt as I began to learn the truth.

Like the woman with the hemorrhaging, I felt like no one or nothing could save me (Mark 5:25-34). I'd been to the psychologists, said "the sinner's prayer," gone through the deliverance services, fasted and prayed, fasted and prayed. Now, for the first time in my life, someone was writing that I was powerless over sin. And, after "Duh!" came, "Whew!" What a relief! There really was something wrong with me! It really wasn't something I could just fix! In fact, it wasn't something anyone around me could fix. Only God could save me! Imagine that.

Many of the authors I was reading were from the 15th to the early 20th century. How could they be the ones who were novel? Maybe it was all the stuff I'd been hearing in the churches before my incarceration that was really new. I had to find out what the Bible said. The churches I attended preached topically, bouncing from one passage to the next. I confess that I'd never read Scripture all the way through. I decided that I should just start at the beginning if I was going to learn anything.

I started in Genesis and read of creation and the fall of man. I read of Eve's temptation—how the tree was "good for food," "pleasant to the eyes," and "able to make one wise." I thought about the passage in I John that states that all that is in the world is the lust of the eyes, the lust of the flesh, and the pride of life, and I began to think that the nature of sin and salvation hadn't changed that much over the years. In fact, it hadn't changed at all. It seemed all of Scripture testified to my wickedness. Following are just a few of the examples I found:

Before the flood, Genesis 6:5 states: "Then the LORD saw that **the wickedness of man was great in the earth, and that every intent of the thoughts of his heart was only evil continually.**"

After the flood, Genesis 8:21 states: ". . . the LORD said in His heart, 'I will never again curse the ground for man's sake, although the imagination of man's heart is evil from his youth.'"

David said, "Behold, I was brought forth in iniquity, and in sin my mother conceived me" (Psalm 51:5).

In Jeremiah 17:9, God said, "The heart is deceitful above all things and desperately wicked."

In Mark 7:21-23, Christ said, "For from within, out of the heart of men, proceed evil thoughts, adulteries, fornications, murders, thefts, covetousness, wickedness, deceit, lewdness, an evil eye, blasphemy, pride, foolishness. All these evil things come from within and defile a man."

In Romans 6:23, Paul stated, ". . .the wages of sin is death, but the gift of God is eternal life in Christ Jesus our Lord."

In Ephesians 2:1-3, Paul wrote, "And you He made alive, who were dead in trespasses and sins, in which you once walked according to the course of this world, according to the prince of the power of the air, the spirit who now works in the sons of disobedience, among whom also we all once conducted ourselves in the lusts of our flesh, fulfilling the desires of the flesh and of the mind, and were by nature children of wrath, just as the others."

With clear statements like these, how could I believe anything else? I was born a sinner and, apart from grace, I will live as a sinner, disobedient, fulfilling my lusts, doing what is right in my own eyes, a child of God's wrath, a dead man walking, deserving of hell.

I was guilty as charged. I am guilty because (1) creation testifies to the true God, yet I exchange His truth for one lie after another (Romans 1:18-23); I am guilty because (2) the law of God and my conscience taught me right from wrong yet I ignore it (Romans 2:12-17); and finally, I am guilty because (3) God's restraining grace doesn't excuse my own wicked intentions any more for me than it did for Abimelech (Genesis 20). Sin corrupts every aspect of my being so that every thought, every intention of my heart, apart from His grace, is only evil, continually. Therefore, I am guilty as charged; guilty on all counts.

And, although I was beginning to see my guilt, God had not yet called me.

"Can the Ethiopian change his skin
or the leopard its spots?
Neither can you do good
who are accustomed to doing evil."
(Jeremiah 13:23)

"I am thankful that I'm incapable
Of doing any good on my own
'Cause we're all stillborn and dead in our transgressions
We're shackled up to the sin we hold so dear."
Excerpted from Thankful by Caedmon's Call

1. Do you believe you that sin has totally corrupted every part of your being so that, apart from grace, every thought, every intention of your heart is only, continually? In other words, do you believe you are *totally* depraved?

    _____

    _____

    _____

2. Are you guilty of what brought you to prison?

    _____

    _____

    _____

3. Do you believe *a* judge or *the* Judge sentenced you to prison?

    _____

    _____

    _____

4. Even if innocent of the crime(s) with which you are charged—whether truly innocent or merely on some technicality—do you now see that you stand guilty of sin before God?

    _____

    _____

    _____

5. What are some of the ways in which you have worshipped the creature instead of the Creator?

    _____

    _____

    _____

6. What are some ways in which you have exchanged His truth for lies? Give examples.

    _____

    _____

    _____

7. Are you able to recognize times in your life at which God may have restrained you from being as bad as you could have been?

    _____

    _____

    _____

8. Do you confess that you are guilty as charged?

    _____

    _____

    _____

9. If you have been hiding behind a technicality and not re-ally dealing with the sin that brought you to prison, confess your sin to God. Like the Pharisee, you can never be right with God until you see your need for the Savior (Luke 18:9-14). The bad news is that, if we say we have no sin, we are liars and His truth is not in us (I John 1:10). The good news of the gospel is that if we confess our sins, He is faithful and just to forgive us (I John 1:9).

    _____

    _____

    _____

NOTES

_____

_____

_____

_____

_____

_____

CHAPTER SEVEN: THE MOMENT OF TRUTH

My mother wrote maybe twice the entire time I was in (we spoke more on the phone when I called collect). The same pastor who met with my fiancé and me before my incarceration faithfully wrote and even sent me money for quite some time. But he no doubt he began to feel used and even he stopped writing me. That was the end of my mail call for a while. When Mount Zion began to inundate me with literature, they became my only hope for mail, and my days seemed to revolve around the next piece of literature they would send. As in Isaiah 6, the United States Postal Service would be my seraph, bringing the coal that would take away my sin! Dr. Robert Morey, a great defender of the faith and the author of a book called *Studies in the Atonement* was the coal![3]

Morey introduced his book by stating that the purpose of Christ's coming was to atone for my sins. Therefore, the degree to which I understand the Atonement is the degree to which I may say I know Christ. In the churches I attended, I can honestly say I am not even sure I remember hearing the word "atonement." He set forth the case for the necessity of Christ's work and the effect it has in the life of a believer. As he demonstrated

---

3   By referring to Dr. Morey as the coal, I certainly do not mean to imply that it was he who took away my sin. I am sure even he would cry out, "Perish the thought!" were I to infer such. Yet, in giving honor where honor is due, it cannot be denied that God used his writing to convict me of sin. For how would I have heard without a preacher? And with regard to Mount Zion and the USPS, how shall a preacher go unless he is sent?

from Scripture what the work of Christ must accomplish, page after page convicted me that I was still in my sin. I began to understand that the work of Christ in the heart of a believer must effect lasting change—not immediate perfection, certainly not in this lifetime anyway—but there must be some evidence of a change in the heart and mind that results in a change in behavior. There must be more than just a confession, more than just a statement of faith, more than just a form of godliness, but a real turning from sin, to God.

I finished the book in a week, late in the fall of 1993. The evening I finished the last chapter, I fell on my bed in tears and cried out to God, "I don't know you, Lord. All these years I have been so certain, but how can I say I know you and be in this place? So here's what I am going to do: I am going to throw out everything I have ever believed and I am going to start over with this book and the Bible. I am going to go through this book and I am either going to prove him wrong or be converted." That night, the gospel had come to me. But that wasn't the first time I'd heard the call. Or was it?

"Woe is me! For I am lost; for I am a man of unclean lips and I dwell in the land of a people of unclean lips, for my eyes have seen the King, the Lord of Hosts!" (Isaiah 6:5). That's what Isaiah's reaction was when he came face-to-face with the holiness of God. By now, these were my sentiments exactly; yet I was still in my sin. The good news, however, comes in the next verse: "Behold, your sin is taken away and your guilt atoned for." Having shown me my sin, God was not going to leave me in it!

CHAPTER EIGHT: FREE AT LAST!

The moment I cried out to God, I believe several stages of my redemption occurred within a very short period of time of each other, if not all at once. First, God called me; the Spirit infused the gospel with the power to save me. The Spirit regenerated me—taking out my heart of stone that refused to obey Him, He gave me a heart of flesh that desired to obey Him. God gave me faith—the ability to believe, agree, trust (rely and act on) what I was reading. I repented—my thinking was changed as I realized I could no longer save myself and must be saved by Christ or I would surely perish. And I was converted; I became a Christian.

I do not believe I became a Christian when I prayed with the pastor as a teenager because (1) I was blinded to the extent of my sinful depravity, (2) I hadn't yet learned that I couldn't save myself, (3) there had been no confession of sin or of Christ as my Savior in that prayer and (4) all of this was evidenced in that I was still completely enslaved to my sin. I couldn't stop sinning.

Still, I had surely heard the gospel many times after that. So what made the prayer I prayed in prison different from the prayer I prayed as a teenager? Or what made the words of Dr. Morey's book different from all the other times I'd heard the gospel? This time, the gospel had come to me in the power of the Holy Spirit! At last, God's call was given; His word cannot return void, it never fails to accomplish the task to which it is sent (Isaiah 55:11)!

The Bible makes a distinction between when the gospel is proclaimed by mere men as opposed to when it is proclaimed with the power of the Holy Spirit. The difference is not so much in the man or even the message; it is in whether the power and presence of God are present to give life to the words. When the message is not to blame and the words are sound, the Scripture distinguishes between what some theologians have called the "gospel call" and the "effectual call."

The gospel call is extended to all, whenever, wherever, and however the gospel is presented; the effectual call occurs only when the message of the cross is infused with the power of the Holy Spirit and faith is gifted by God in the heart of the one being called.[4] For example, I am called to preach to all but it is clear that not all will believe. Why do some believe whereas others refuse? Both heard the same message, but change only comes to the one who has been "born again" or, said another way, regenerated.

Remember when Nicodemus told Christ he wanted to be "born again"? It's a wonder Christ didn't stop right then and lead Nicodemus in a sinner's prayer! Boy, he blew it then, didn't he? If salvation is dependent on the free will of man, never has a man been more "willing" than Nicodemus. He asked the question every preacher longs to hear, "How can a man be born when he is old?" (John 3:4). How did Christ answer? "The wind blows where it wishes, and you hear the sound of it, but cannot tell where it comes from or where it goes. So it is with everyone who is born of the Spirit" (John 3:8). In other words, **Christ was telling Nicodemus that he could talk to him until he was blue in the face but the words would simply fall on deaf ears without the Spirit's work!**

Paul wrote that the work of the Spirit gave him confidence to preach in the first place. He said that the disciples preached to

---

4   See John 3:16 vs. I Thessalonians 1:5-9.

all. To some the words became the aroma of life leading to life, to others they were the aroma of death leading to death (2 Corinthians 2: 12-17). Who or what makes the difference? Why do some believe and others refuse? Why had I refused for so long and just now believed? Paul said it is God who makes the call. Christ said, "*This* is the work of God: that you believe in Him who was sent" (John 6:29, emphasis added). Paul wrote, "For by grace you have been saved through faith, not of yourselves, it is the gift of God, not of works, lest anyone should boast" (Ephesians 2:8). "It" is faith. Faith is the gift of God.

Faith comes by hearing and hearing by the Word (Romans 10:17). With the heart man believes, and with the mouth confession is made to salvation (Romans 10:9, 10). But why believe and confess then when I had previously refused? What made the gospel take hold of me then? How is it that I came to believe the Word this time? Some plant, others water, but God causes the seed to grow (I Corinthians 3:6). Humbling, isn't it? God makes the difference. Specifically, the Spirit makes the difference. **A flashlight is just a conduit for light. Without the batteries, the flashlight is worthless. Without the Spirit, the message of the Cross is foolishness to the listener.** So once the Spirit of God chose to regenerate me, what happened next?

I repented.

Repent comes from the Greek words *meta*, which means after, and *noeo*, which refers to the mind. It literally means to change my mind, to change my thinking. What changed? Repentance began when I believed I was a sinner. Indeed, not just a sinner, but the worst of sinners. I wasn't a victim; I was a victimizer. I was an enemy of God. I was disobedient. I conducted myself according to my lusts. I was a child of wrath. I was dead in my sins.

If I am honest, the reality of that those truths had never gripped my heart before. I acknowledged that we are all born into sin. In some ways, I may even have believed that I was guilty of having sinned. After all, everyone makes mistakes. Never before had I come to believe that I was a sinner. I was the one sinning. I was an enemy of God. I resisted the evidence in creation. I resisted His law written on my heart. I resisted His Word. I exchanged His truths for lie after lie. I was a worshipper of Satan.

Wait a minute, you say, that's going too far! You didn't really worship Satan . . . did you? Yes. So does that mean I wore all black, read from the Satanic Bible, practiced human sacrifice, and consciously pledged my devotion to Lucifer, the Prince of Darkness? No. But the whole of my life was oriented toward the sin I desired. As Paul wrote in Ephesians 2, I went through life fulfilling the lusts of my flesh, following Satan, the prince of the air. I worshipped the devil. I would even go so far as to say I sometimes still do. We all do. There is no such thing as neutrality in life. Either I worship God or I am worshipping the devil. Either I am with Christ or I am against Him. Either I obey Him or I am obeying the prince of the power of the air. Let that sink in for a moment. Whom are you worshipping?

So the gospel was proclaimed, the Spirit infused the message with life-changing power, and I repented. I changed my mind. I had a change in my thinking. I am no longer the victim; I am the victimizer. I am a sinner; I sin. No one made me sin. No one makes me sin. I do it naturally, even proficiently. Now what? Now comes the judgment. For, if I believe I am a sinner, then I must also believe that the wages of sin is death (Romans 6:23). The Scripture says, "If God is for us, who can be against us?" But the converse is true also, "The Lord will not leave the guilty unpunished. . . . Who can withstand His indignation? Who can endure His fierce anger?" (Nahum 1:1-6). God knows, not me!

God knows I don't deserve His grace. In *The Sovereignty of God*, Arthur Pink wrote that some define grace as unmerited favor. He said that definition doesn't do justice to the grace of God. Pink said if a beggar asks me for a dollar and I give it to him, that's unmerited favor. He didn't do anything to earn it; he didn't deserve it. But if a man beats me, robs me, and leaves me for dead, and then one day finds himself in a position in which he needs my help and I give it to him, that is closer to the meaning of grace. It's not merely *un*merited favor; it's *de*-merited favor. It's not that I haven't earned it; it's that I was an enemy of God. By almost anyone's standards, I really was chief of sinners. In the eyes of men, and perhaps even in the eyes of God, there was no worse sin. I sinned against His most precious creation. Were it not for grace, it would have been better if a millstone had been hung around my neck and I had been thrown into the ocean (Luke 17:2). As the Scripture says:

"It is fearful thing to fall into the hands of an angry, living God."
(Hebrews 10:31)

That night, I believed I was a sinner. I didn't deserve mercy; I deserved judgment. I was worthy of death. I deserved death. I knew I couldn't change myself. The trail of my victims and the walls of stone and razor wire that surrounded me then stood as a grim reminder of that fact. I couldn't imagine why God would want to save me. Like the infamous tax collector, another sinner reviled, justly under a sentence of death for his sins, I had only one option left: cast myself down at His feet and beg for undeserved mercy!

"To some who were confident of their own righteousness and looked down on everybody else, Jesus told this parable: 'Two men went up to the temple to pray, one a Pharisee and the other a tax collector. The Pharisee stood up and prayed about himself: "God, I thank you that I am not like other men—robbers, evildoers, adulterers—or even like this tax collector. I fast twice a week and give a tenth of all I get." But the tax collector stood at a distance. He would not even look up to heaven, but beat his breast and said, "God, have mercy on me, a sinner." I tell you that this man, rather than the other, went home justified before God. For everyone who exalts himself will be humbled, and he who humbles himself will be exalted.'" (Luke 18:9-14)

I had come to realize that I had been playing the Pharisee my whole life. I trusted in everything and everyone to save me except Christ. The state tried to change me; I tried to change myself. Hands were laid on me and devils were supposedly cast out of me, but I was still very much possessed. I wasn't possessed by a demon; I was possessed by the lusts of my own flesh (James 1:14). I was doing what was right in my own eyes.

That night, however, the good news was that I had become the tax collector. The Word of God, empowered by the Spirit, changed me. I now realized I was a sinner. I could not save myself. I deserved death. My only hope was in the mercy and grace of God. And, as Dr. Morey wrote in *Studies in the Atonement*, ". . . conversion flows from FAITH for we read that they 'turned to God' (verse 9). And conversion flows out of REPENTANCE for they 'turned from idols' (verse 9)." Consequently, this time I was converted. Imagine that! I failed to find God when I was free but He found me while I was in prison!

***

Later, I was sitting in the dorms reading *The Institutes of the Christian Religion* when I read a statement Calvin made that I couldn't believe. **Calvin wrote that God often uses circumstances others might call evil to draw men to Himself**. He cited Psalm 107 as his proof text. The Psalm describes how God used famine in the desert, sickness and disease, storms at sea, wealth, poverty, and even prison to bring men to Himself! Let's break down verses 10 through 15:

> *"Those who sat in darkness and in the shadow of death,*
> *Bound in affliction and irons--*
> *Because they rebelled against the words of God,*
> *And despised the counsel of the Most High. . ."*

The state sentenced me to prison for my crimes, and justifiably so, for the Scripture declares that the state exists to be a terror to those who commit evil (Romans 13:3). I was undoubtedly in prison because I was a sinner, even the chief of sinners. But what they clearly intended for evil as a punishment for my sin, God intended for my good! He caused me to be "carried away captive" that He might save me!

"Therefore He brought down their heart with labor;
They fell down, and there was none to help.
Then they cried out to the LORD in their trouble,
And He saved them out of their distresses."

God put me in prison to break me. I only cried out to God when I found myself in the worst trouble of my life. I had no one else to help. That's when I cried out to God, and that's when He saved me!

"He brought them out of darkness and the shadow of death,
And broke their chains in pieces.
Oh, that men would give thanks to the LORD for His goodness,
And for His wonderful works to the children of men!"

God gave me a freedom from sin I had never known while still in prison, and that more abundantly after I was released!

Four times the Psalmist sings, "Oh, that men would give thanks to the LORD for His goodness, and for His wonderful works to the children of men!" What were His wonderful works to me? He allowed me to be carried away captive that He might save me! In Romans 8:28, Paul wrote, "And we know that all things work together for good to those who love God, to those who are called according to His purposes." Note, Paul didn't write, "to those who love God *and* to those who are called." He was qualifying the phrase before with the statement after. I love God because He called me according to His purposes. Over and over again, the Psalmist declares, **God is at work in my life, even during the hardest times, driving me to my knees to show me my need of Him.**

Remember when the wind and the waves rocked the boat and the disciples called out, "'Teacher, do you not care that we are perishing?' Christ stood up and said, 'Peace, be still!' and the wind ceased and there was a great calm," (Mark 4:35-41). It was the perfect picture of how God saved me and many others. Our sins lead us into the darkness of a storm; we can't save ourselves and no one is around who can. Then we call out to God, and He saves us! Oh, I give thanks to you Lord for your wonderful work in me! I give thanks for your irresistible grace!

Those who reject the total depravity of man will, of course, see this as an unkind caricature of God. "Whoever is wise will observe these things," however, "and they will understand the loving kindness of the LORD" (Psalm 107:43).

I knew then that prison was absolutely God's will for my life. If I had any doubts before, this passage cleared them all away. The absolute, amazing, humbling fact of it all was that prison was more than just God's righteous and holy judgment of my sin, it was also the way He was calling me to Himself. My captivity was to give me the first real freedom I'd ever known. Change had come!

***

The Bible teaches that, when God changes your thinking, you will live differently.[5] As a man thinks in his heart, so is he, is true for sinners and saints alike (Proverbs 23:7). Out of the heart flow the issues of life (Proverbs 4:23). A true change in my thinking could not help but lead to a change in my behavior.

"For our gospel did not come to you in word only, but also in power . . . you became followers of us and of the Lord, having received the word in much affliction, with joy of the Holy Spirit, so that you became examples to all. . . . For they themselves declare concerning us what manner of entry we had to you, and how you turned to God from idols to serve the living and true God." (I Thessalonians 1:5-9)

---

5   Some might say that I am overemphasizing the role of my mind in salvation. They might ask, "What about the heart?" I think this comes from a faulty understanding of Scripture and the nature of men. I know there are many who believe men are (1) body, (2) soul (aka mind), and (3) spirit (or heart), but the truth of the Scripture is that we are really dualistic beings: body and spirit. In the Scripture, the words flesh and mind and soul and spirit are used fairly interchangeably. We are material, we have a body; and we are immaterial, we have a soul (or spirit). So when I say I repented, I had a change of mind, I am really saying I had a change of heart, and I have already stated that this was the work of the Spirit.

Paul said that the faith of the Thessalonians was known all around. What evidence did he offer that this was true? How did Paul, writing under the inspiration of the Holy Spirit, judge their faith to be genuine? It was not their words but their repentance. It was that they "turned from idols to serve the living and the true God." To what or whom did Paul credit this change? Verse 4 states it was the power of the Holy Spirit.

Steven Curtis Chapman wrote a song that asks the question, "What about the change?" He speaks of having all the signs of being a Christian—the WWJD bracelet, the Scripture magnets on his refrigerator door, and a Jesus bumper sticker on his car, but, he asks, "What about the change? What about the difference? What about the grace? What about forgiveness? What about a life that's showing I'm undergoing the change? . . . I want to live a life that's showing, I'm undergoing the change."

Repentance began for me with this most basic confession: God, be merciful to me, a sinner. Repentance continues as I begin to learn how to think God's thoughts after Him, how to think Biblically, how to replace old, sinful habits with new, righteous patterns of behavior, how to be transformed in the renewing of my mind, how to put off the old man and to put on the new. Growth in sanctification occurs as more and more distance is placed between me and my sin, as my soul is purified in obeying the truth. (See Romans 12:1,2; Ephesians 4:20-32; I Peter 1:22.)

Skip Ryan, professor of practical theology and Chancellor at Redeemer Theological Seminary in Dallas, Texas, sums it up this way: **"The truth is that we are far worse sinners than we could ever imagine, but that we are far more loved by God than we could ever conceive and, at the intersection of those two truths in the heart, the gospel explodes upon the scene and we are changed!"**

It was clear my heart had been changed but, if I was to grow in sanctification, further repentance was necessary regarding the excuses I had been using for my sin.

""Why was I made to hear Thy voice,
And enter while there's room,
When thousands make a wretched choice,
And rather starve than come?""

Excerpted from *How Sweet and Awful is the Place*
by Issac Watts

"How deep the Father's love for us
How vast beyond all measure
That He should give His only Son
And make a wretch His treasure."

Excerpted from *How Deep the Father's Love for Us*
by Stuart Townend

1. Are you lost? Explain your answer.

   _____

   _____

   _____

2. If you are saved, who or what has made you clean, and how?

   _____

   _____

   _____

3. Define the word atonement.

   _____

   _____

   _____

4. If God was to be just and the justifier of the one who places faith in Christ, was the death of Christ really necessary? Did it have to happen that way? Was there another way?

_____

_____

_____

_____

5. The author states that the work of Christ must produce lasting change. Do you agree or disagree with this statement. Why or why not?

_____

_____

_____

_____

6. The author states that salvation is absolutely dependent on the work of the Spirit in the heart *before* one is able to believe. Do you agree with this statement?

_____

_____

_____

7. What does it mean to repent?

_____

_____

_____

_____

8. The author states that all of life is worship in one direction or another; either we are worshipping Christ or we are worshipping Satan. Do you agree with this statement?

_____

_____

_____

9. Whom are you worshipping?

_____

_____

_____

10. In your own words, explain the difference between the Pharisee and the tax collector. Why did the tax collector go home justified? What does it mean that the Pharisee did not? Had both walked out and dropped dead, where do you believe each would have spent eternity?

_____

_____

_____

11. The author states that he did what was right in his own eyes. This is actually repeated many times in reference to the children of Israel throughout the book of Judges (e.g., Judges 17:6). Everyone does what is right in his or her own eyes. Is that really wrong? Why or why not?

_____

_____

_____

12. It has been said that the definition of insanity is to keep doing the same thing expecting different results. Do you believe you *must* stop doing what is right in your own eyes?

_____

_____

_____

13. Do you believe it's God's will you're in prison? Why or why not?

_____

_____

_____

14. In Psalm 107:10-15, when does it say that the prisoners cried out to the Lord?

_____

_____

_____

15. Do you believe prison is the means God has chosen to save you? Why or why not?

_____

_____

_____

16. Where do you learn how to replace sinful with righteous habits?

_____

_____

_____

17. From where or whom does your help come?

_____

_____

_____

NOTES

_____

_____

_____

_____

_____

_____

_____

_____

_____

_____

_____

_____

_____

_____

_____

_____

CHAPTER NINE: NO SPECIAL CASES

After more than two years of God revealing to me the wickedness of my heart and His sovereignty in my salvation, I guess He thought it was time for me to graduate (Hebrews 5:12—6:3). I was transferred from Jackie Brannon to Jess Dunn Correctional Center, where I would serve the rest of my sentence.

Not long after I arrived, the doctrines I was learning and teaching to others became known to many on the yard. The chaplain's clerk, another inmate, said that he knew someone he thought I should meet. In prison for his own sins, "Joe" was leading a weekly Bible study, which I began to attend. More than anything else, I was drawn to his ability to open up the Scripture and apply it to life.

Once during our study, I told Joe of my dream to start a 12-step approach for people who struggled with sexual sin. Joe looked me in the eye and said, "Chandler, what you're learning applies to more than just salvation. It's an entire world and life view, a way of interpreting all of life through the lenses of Scripture." I asked him what he meant, and he answered by introducing me to some great books.

The most significant of these was *Competent to Counsel* by Jay E. Adams. This was the first book Jay wrote on the subject of Biblical counseling. It was written in 1970; the year I was born. It was the way Adams exposited I Corinthians 10:13 that began to make it possible for me to see measurable progress in turning from my sin to serve Christ. Adams made two points about this passage that then and now are largely responsible for growth in my own sanctification. Let's look at the verse:

"No temptation has overtaken you except such as is common to man; but God is faithful, who will not allow you to be tempted beyond what you are able, but with the temptation will also make the way of escape, that you may be able to bear it."
(I Corinthians 10:13)

1.) *No temptation has overtaken me that's not common to man.* **Adams wrote, "God allows no Christian to plead that his case is special or unique."** This had been and, if I am honest, sometimes still is the excuse I use for my sin. "But you don't understand! I've been this way far too long. This sin is different. It's stronger. It's too deeply rooted. I can't change." Adams rebuked such thinking by stating that this passage says that **Christians can't say "can't" because God says they can. Whenever I say "can't," I am calling God a liar.**

2.) *God is faithful.* The reason we can't say can't, Adams continued, is that "temptations and tests are tailor-made to each individual; and God is the tailor!" **Our ability to resist temptation is not based on our own ability, but on God's character and faithfulness.** In other words, I must accept the promises of God based on His strength and ability and not my own! My ability to resist sin is guaranteed by the very nature and character of God's Word. He's promised He won't place any more on me than I can stand. Not because I can stand on my own, but because when I am weak He is strong on my behalf!

Jay went on to describe that we become enslaved to sin through habituation. First we learn what pleases our sinful desires, then we sin to get it; soon we orient ourselves around that sin. This is why Christ said that we can't love God and money. One will give way to the other. He said, "The lamp of the body is the eye" (Matthew 6:19-24). In other words, what we think and understand about the world around us determines how we live.

So, in reference to God's promise to provide the way of escape, Jay made the following point:

> *3.) Everything we need to love God and our neighbor is found in Scripture.* Every way of escape, everything we need to "stand up under" or resist temptation is found in The Book. **For every sin, there is a pattern of righteousness that should replace it.** Let the thief who stole steal no more; let him go to work so that he will have to give to others. He stole before; now he should give.

Which begs the question, what is the Biblical pattern of righteousness to combat sexual immorality? According to Scripture, the primary combatant to sexual immorality is marriage:

> *". . . because of sexual immorality, let each man have his own wife, and let each woman have her own husband."*
> *(I Corinthians 7:2)*

But how could I hope for marriage when I wasn't yet attracted to women?

1. In your own words, break down and explain the meaning of I Corinthians 10:13.

   _____

   _____

   _____

2. Do you believe God "tailor" makes every test you face? Why or why not?

   _____

   _____

3. Do you see your ability to resist sin as being dependent on you—your faith, your works, your diligence, or whatever, or do you see it as being dependent on God?

4. What sinful patterns brought you to prison? What righteous patterns should replace them?

5. Do you recognize that being in church, reading your Bible, even praying, means little apart from turning from sin? Obedience is better than sacrifice.

6. Whose power must you have if you are to turn from sin and break the chains that have held you for so long?

CHAPTER TEN: A FUTURE AND A HOPE

I was learning so much from Joe, but I knew *I* needed to learn to study for myself as well (2 Timothy 2:15). One day I was reading in Jeremiah and became frustrated. In God's providence, I stopped at Chapter 28, fell on my bed, and began to pray, "God, why can't I get out of Your Word what Joe does? Why doesn't Your Word come alive to me the way it does for him? You said that if I lacked wisdom I could ask. Well, I'm asking." When I opened the Scripture the next day, the Word leapt off the page and into my heart! You probably know the passage to which I'm referring. It's quoted in church, engraved on Christian trinkets, and often cited in prayer.

> *"For I know the thoughts that I think toward you, says the LORD, thoughts of peace and not of evil, to give you a future and a hope. Then you will call upon Me and go and pray to Me, and I will listen to you." (Jeremiah 29:11-13)*

The passage is frequently used to offer hope to the hopeless, and well it should be! The context is too often ignored or passed over, however. The book of Jeremiah gives the account of a rebellious Israel, God's constant pleading with them to repent, His warning of impending judgment, consequences of captivity if they didn't, the false prophets who arose to say otherwise, and the promise of Israel's redemption and deliverance. Jeremiah was about men, women, and children who had been taken captive for their sin. They were, in a manner of speaking, in prison!

Wow! What was God trying to tell me?

Literal Verse	Application
"Build houses and settle down," v. 5	Decorate my cell, sit down, shut up, and get used to it! I'm going to be here a while.
"plant gardens and eat what they produce," v. 5	Work on my heart while I'm here. Pray. Study. Fellowship. Build on the foundation Christ has laid. Get an education. Learn a trade.
"Take wives and beget sons and daughters," v. 6	Seek the forgiveness of those against whom I sinned. Start setting my mind on Christ's desire for my life—to seek a wife. Start praying for her, for our children, for us, now.
"seek the peace and prosperity of the city," v. 7	As much as is within me, strive to live peaceably with all men.
"Pray to the Lord for it," v. 7	Pray for my cellmate, the rest of the prison, the administration and the warden, my country, my president.
". . . have spoken lying words in My name, which I have not commanded them," v. 23	Stop believing the lies of those who try to tell me that prison isn't God's will for my life. Stop looking for ways to escape God's judgment on a technicality in the court system.

God introduced His message to the captives in this way: "Thus says the LORD of hosts, the God of Israel, to all who were carried away captive, whom I have caused to be carried away from Jerusalem to Babylon . . ." (Jeremiah 29:4; see also 29:7, 14, 18, 20). Not once, but more than five times in this chapter, God declared that He caused Israel to be taken captive. He led the armies of Babylon, not the king! Just as assuredly as God used the Babylonian captivity to bring His people to repentance, **He used prison to draw me to Himself (John 6:65).**

Time and again the prophets pleaded with the children of Israel to repent. Time and again they refused. God said enough is enough. He caused the Babylonians to take them captive. He sentenced them to 70 years of captivity. Despite the false prophets who would come along and say their captivity wasn't God's will, in Jeremiah 29, God tells them to get used to it: build houses, plant gardens, take wives and have kids. You're going to be here a while; 70 years to be exact. But as it so often is with God, right in the middle of the bad news is the good. After their time is served, they will cry out to God and He will save them. For He knows the plans that He has for them: their captivity is to give them the first real freedom they've ever known. God will restore them to a life they could never have imagined apart from His grace. Jeremiah 29:11 meant hope for me, and hope was something I thought I'd lost forever.

Before my incarceration, there had been periods in my life of great prosperity. Even without a college degree and in spite of my sin, God had extended much common grace to me over the years. It had just been weeks before my arrest that I was hired by a financial planning firm, and only days before that I had passed the exams for my insurance licenses once again. Because of God's restraining grace, through my relationship with my fiancé and her children, and again in spite of my sin, I had experienced a foretaste of what a real family might look like. Now it was all gone; I had lost everything.

I sinned against God and His most precious creation. There had been many opportunities to repent. I refused them all and continued in my sin. I made it worse by trying to save myself. So God caused the State of Oklahoma to carry me away captive. But then He sent His Word to me. And at the appointed time, I cried out to Him and He saved me! Now He was promising me that my captivity was to result in the only real freedom I had ever known. He gave me hope—real hope, hope that cannot disappoint because it is based on His nature, character and Word. He said He had good plans for me, plans for a future with Him. Thirteen years later, I know this to have been a hope that did not disappoint. And it just gets better, for I also know I am experiencing only a foretaste of what's to come!

In this hope I was being saved but hope that is seen is not hope (Romans 8:24). I would have to wait for it with patience (Romans 8:25). And patience had never been a strong suit for me!

Thinking of this hope, I half-heartedly commented to Joe, "Wouldn't it give God such glory if He made me celibate and I . . . well, I just lived happily ever after." Joe looked me straight in the eye and answered, "No, Chandler, what would give God more glory is to make you into the husband and father He created you to be."

As Abraham had when he first heard the promise of God to give him a son, I laughed, said "Sure," and walked away (Genesis 17:17). But what I should have done is be silent.

Read Jeremiah 29.

1. Why were the children of Israel taken captive? What was their crime?

2. For how long were they sentenced?

3. Who was responsible for their captivity?

4. What were the false prophets saying? Whose counsel were they to avoid? Why?

5. What did God say MUST happen before He would save and restore them?

6. What did God say He would do if they would seek Him?

7. What did God say would happen to all those who said otherwise?

8. Challenge question: What did God say would happen to the Babylonians because they took Israel captive, even though God is said to have caused it, and why?

_____

_____

_____

9. Do you believe it is God's will that you're in prison?

_____

_____

_____

10. What is God's will for you while you're here?

_____

_____

_____

11. What should you be doing?

_____

_____

_____

12. Are you doing it? (If not, tell the group what, by God's grace, you're committing to begin doing.)

_____

_____

_____

13. What has God promised to you if you will seek Him now?

_____

_____

_____

NOTES

_____

_____

_____

_____

_____

_____

_____

_____

_____

_____

_____

_____

_____

_____

CHAPTER ELEVEN:
THE RIGHT TO REMAIN SILENT

I have always been a talker. From having a "schizophrenic" mother to being raised in group homes and being on my own, I learned how to be independent. **Prior to becoming a Christian, I believed the only way I was going to get what I wanted was if I used, abused, and manipulated everyone and everything around me toward that end.** So I learned how to communicate well enough to get whatever I wanted.

The state may not have given me a loving home with a mom or dad, but I had food, clothes, and a roof over my head. The group homes had plumbing, heating, air conditioning, even cable television! I certainly had more than many others throughout the world. But self-reliance naturally produces self-centeredness, and because I was the only one who cared about me, my wants and needs were the only ones that mattered. According to Scripture, however, what I want is the product of the thoughts and intents of a heart that is "only evil continually" (Genesis 6:5). Hence, my own thoughts and desires could not be trusted.

What I was learning about true Christianity was that, in the grand scheme of things, I really didn't matter. God's will is all that matters. He doesn't need me, as He himself gives life and breath to all (Acts 17:25). In the words "Who Am I," the song by Casting Crowns, "I am a flower quickly fading, here today and gone tomorrow, a wave tossed in the ocean, a vapor in the wind" (the lyrics of which are largely reminiscent of I Peter 1:24-25).

By the time I was really converted, I had just less than 24 years of learning how to think and orient my life around sin and self. I think it's safe to say that anyone will become proficient at anything he or she does for that long. I was good at sinning. It was all I knew. I was fast to speak and slow to listen because that was how I learned to get what I wanted. I fully expect that it's going to take the rest of my life to undo the first years of my life. Sometimes it feels as if I am taking a teaspoon to a mountain of sin. **The more I know about God, the more I realize how great a sinner I am.**

In *The Pursuit of Holiness*, Jerry Bridges remarked that one feels closest to God at the moment he or she is converted. As I learn more, however, I begin to see myself as moving farther and farther away from God. The reason is that, as my knowledge of God's holiness grows, so does my understanding as to the depth of my depravity. The more I grow, the more I see my need for a Savior.

The first time I heard the words directed at me, "You have the right to remain silent," I was being arrested. Now it was as if God was arresting my heart. The more I learn about my sin, the more I realize that the best thing I can do is to stop being so independent, keep my mouth shut, and stop making my own decisions. Because I am surrounded by so great a cloud of witnesses, I need to start to depend on Him and the means of grace He provides (Hebrews 12:1, 2). **I need to surround myself with men wiser than I am,** men who have spent the better part of their lives serving and obeying God instead of rebelling.

Very soon I would be in the free world again. I had a long history of making horrible decisions. I had been trying to turn from sin on my own for many years, and prison is where that ended. "There is a way that seems right to man but its end is the way of death" (Proverbs 14:12). That's why the Scripture teaches:

> *"For by wise counsel you will wage your own war,*
> *and in a multitude of counselors **there is safety.**"*
> *(Proverbs 24:6, emphasis added.)*

After so many years of sin, I needed that multitude of counselors! This begged the question, however: Where would I attend church?

Prior to my incarceration, I attended churches and consulted with pastors from many different denominations. None of them offered me "the words of eternal life." It's not a question of whether they might have eventually; it may even have been that I was just too blinded by my sin to see what was right in front of me. Regardless, God had not been pleased to reveal Himself to me in any of those churches. He revealed Himself to me in the treasure of Reformation theology. Where else could I go except to a church that believed the same truths that had begun to change my life? The Apostle Peter knew the right answer.

After Christ told a few of his followers what was in store for Him and for them, several of them left. Christ asked Peter, "Do you want to go away as well?" Albeit in a different context, Peter answered, "Lord, to whom shall we go? You have the words of eternal life, and we have believed and have to come to know that you are the Holy One of God." (John 6:68-69)

So I asked Joe, "Who teaches this stuff? Where should I attend church after my release?" He suggested that I write the Orthodox Presbyterian Church (OPC) and ask them for a directory. They sent me one and encouraged me to begin to try to establish contact with a church in my area. The only problem was that there were only two OPC churches in Oklahoma. One was in Oklahoma City, and the other was in Bartlesville. Both were considerably far from Jess Dunn.

Nevertheless, I began to write these churches and others I knew to "speak the same things" (I Corinthians 1:10). I was pleading for someone to visit and disciple me while I was still in prison and for a church to come alongside and help me when I got out. I wrote to so many I lost count—and some more than once. A few months later, I decided to try a more aggressive approach: I called collect. One pastor finally responded. Richard

Shaw, then pastor of Bartlesville OPC, began to drive 200 miles to visit me every month for the last couple of years I was in prison.

Eventually, to prepare me for membership, Pastor Shaw began to walk me through *Confessing Christ* by Calvin Cummings. After he learned that I was planning on attending Oklahoma State University (OSU) at Stillwater upon my release, he contacted the Reformed Presbyterian Church of North America in Stillwater to ask whether they would be willing to provide assistance to me upon my release and, eventually, to receive me as a member.

The pastor, Bruce Parnell, encouraged Pastor Shaw to have me call. As soon as I did, I learned the session had already met and decided they wanted to help. I remember Pastor Parnell saying something to the effect of, "Uh, Chandler, it's not every day I get a call like this. What did you have in mind? How can we help?" I explained that I was planning to attend OSU and I also believed I already had a job lined up. So I asked, "Would it be possible for the church to help me get a room at a weekly motel until I could receive my first paycheck?" And Pastor Parnell said he thought that would be a great idea!

Over the next couple of weeks I spoke to the pastors with greater frequency. Then, four years after I had arrived in prison—December 5, 1996—I walked out of Jess Dunn Correctional Center a free man. Free from sin but not yet free from the consequences of my sin, for now I would begin the sentence of probation I'd received at the same time I had been sentenced to prison. Sam Bates, a Prison Fellowship volunteer from Asbury United Methodist Church in Tulsa, Oklahoma, was there to pick me up.

The day I was scheduled to leave I was afraid something would come up and we wouldn't make it out of the gate. Even as we drove away, I half held my breath until we had miles between the prison and us. I kept checking the rearview mirror for flashing lights but I calmed down and finally began to believe it was real when we arrived in Stillwater.

We met Pastor Parnell at the weekly motel the church had booked. After the introductions had been made all around, Sam and I said goodbye and Pastor Parnell handed me my key to the hotel room. Then he surprised me by handing me an envelope. He said, "This is a gift from the session. You don't need to worry about paying us back. There's $200 in it. Use it to get whatever you need. You obviously can't live here forever. Tomorrow, we'd like for you to begin looking for a longer-term place to live. The session will help with all your expenses until you can get on your feet. As soon as you're able to find a job, all we ask is that you'll agree to meet with us so we can help you learn how to budget your money." It was late, so we didn't visit long. He said goodbye, and we agreed to meet again the next day.

For the first time in more than four years, I used a key and unlocked the door to my own room. I fell on the bed. After a while, I began to cry. Who was this God who brought these people into my life? Who am I that He should be mindful of me? Who are these people? Why have they been so gracious to me? Doesn't God—don't they—know who I am and what I've done? My heart was filled with gratitude and a desire to please God. Not because I must or I'd go to hell, although that was certainly true, but because I was grateful! This is what the Spirit of grace can do that the letter of the law never could; He gave me a heart that wanted to please God!

It wasn't long before my mind turned to other matters, however. It's a long-standing tradition that most of whatever men have on the inside stays on the inside to be passed on to someone else in need when they leave. I left all my hygiene supplies and most of my literature and canteen with those still inside. Before I could start my day tomorrow, I would need a shower, and I suddenly realized that I didn't have any toiletries or clothes! So I did something else I had not done for more than four years: I got up and walked out the door I had just let myself in! After I walked to Wal-Mart and purchased what I needed, the enjoyment of the cool air on my face had worn off and it occurred to me that it was cold outside! I finally asked someone whether he would give me a ride back to the motel and, not without some reluctance, he agreed.

The next day I was scheduled to report to the Department of Probation and Parole to begin my five-year suspended sentence.

***

Before my release, I became concerned about whether the state might try to impose any requirements for "state approved" counseling. In my youth, I'd already heard from the "professionals," and God knows they didn't have the words of life!

Jay Adams, author of *Competent to Counsel*, *More Than Redemption* and more than a hundred other titles, is also the founder of the Christian Counseling Educational Foundation. Edward T. Welch is a reputable, licensed, CCEF staff psychologist who long ago traded in "what is falsely called science" for the truth of God's word (I Timothy 6:20). Dr. Welch had the credentials I needed to head off any state-imposed requirements. I wrote and asked whether he would agree to oversee the counseling Pastor Parnell would provide, which I hoped would lend credibility to it in the eyes of the state.

When I went to meet with my probation officer for the first time, I held the letter in hand from Dr. Edward Welch. Somewhat taken aback at my preparation for our first meeting, the probation officer accepted it, imposing no additional requirements on me.

***

Prior to my release, I'd also sent a resume to a telemarketing company called VisionQuest Marketing. Surprisingly, the hiring manager wrote back and told me to contact him after I was released. The next morning I showered, put on my new clothes, and went to apply for the job.

In God's providence, VisionQuest was Christian-owned! It was the marketing arm of Lifeline Long Distance, which was an affinity marketing company that donated 10 percent of a bill to the Christian charity of choice. So by my second day out of prison, I had a church home, a place to stay, new clothes, and a new job!

***

The Stillwater RPC met in the basement of a small building. It was made up of fewer than ten families and 50 or so children. Most of the members were on staff at the university or were business owners. All of the kids in the church were home-schooled.

For the first time in my life, I'd made the decision that I was going to learn how to trust others for counsel. I was going to trust the church to which I'd submitted myself and the elders who had been at the work of purifying their souls in obeying the truth far longer than I had. I who had been independent for so long was going to learn how to be dependent on the God who had saved me and the church He gave me. Surprisingly, even to someone who had been in prison, giving up one's independence and learning how to be dependent is harder than it sounds.

I'd spent the last two years of my incarceration preparing to go to college. Imagine my surprise when the church elders suggested that I wait to begin college! If I went to work for a year, I could start the next year as a resident and not be forced to pay out-of-state tuition. This was really hard for me to swallow. I'd worked so hard to find a college willing to accept me. Now they wanted me to wait for what seemed like an eternity! It didn't matter that what they were suggesting made sense; I just wanted to go to college!

It had long been a pattern in my life to do what I wanted, when I wanted, how I wanted, because that was my right. After all, I'm a grown man! Then, I began to think . . . look where that ended. So I swallowed my pride and submitted to their counsel. I began to go to work, meet weekly with the pastor, and pay my bills, and life began to look somewhat normal. Wow!

Then I faced another challenge. As I began to live and pay bills, I decided I should probably clean up some old debts. I ordered a copy of my credit report and found I still had several bad checks I'd written on my report. When I called the businesses, they said I needed to speak with the district attorney. The DA told me I had to pay all of them off, plus court costs, or face being arrested and extradited back to Texas to face charges!

I called the pastor and told him the news. He said he needed some time to consider what should be done. He prayed with me and asked me to trust that God would resolve the matter. Surely, He hadn't brought me this far to send me back to Egypt? So I did. Then I called my "dad," Michael Shelton with Mount Zion, who'd fathered me in the faith. He said, "Chandler, I don't care what it takes, I'll see to it that debt gets paid." When I told my pastor, he smiled at me and said, "Well, tell him if he does that we're in for half." **This church full of people I'd never met, a church that had already shelled out significant sums of money in helping me after my release, and a man I only knew through the mail, thousands of miles away, paid my debt—just as Christ has done for those who will believe!**

I continued to live, work, meet with the pastor, and pay bills. Because I'd not been received as a member of the church, Pastor Parnell began to walk me through an introduction to the faith. We finished the book one week before I was to make a profession of my faith to the church, but this week was communion. Pastor Parnell looked at me and said, "Chandler, since we haven't had a chance to meet with you regarding your confession of faith, the session would ask that you refrain from taking communion this week."

"Oh, I am so sure! I've been in the church, with your families, in your homes, walked among you, submitted when you asked me not to go to school, and you want me not to take communion! Are you kidding me?" I said.

Pastor Parnell tried to calm me down, but I wasn't having any of it.

Taking communion was my right!

"Well, I'll tell you what: you have your little communion service. I won't be there. I'll find another place to worship this Sunday," and so I did.

I worshipped with a Christian Missionary Alliance congregation. I can't remember how I met the pastor but, given my new-found theology and—now I'd say lack of humility—I felt like it was the only church I could tolerate. Was I ever in for it!

The pastor preached on an often-overlooked phrase in Philippians 2:6. Paul wrote that, although Christ was in the very form of God, He did not count equality with God something to be grasped, but made Himself nothing, taking the form of a servant. The pastor said he wanted to focus that week on the phrase "something to be grasped." He said that this might be better translated "something to hold onto or defend." In other words, although Christ was God in heaven, He didn't count the associated privileges as rights to which He could not let go. Instead, He willingly relinquished the privileges and took on the form of a servant.

I think one of the best illustrations of this is seen in Mark Twain's *The Prince and the Pauper.* While the story can only be applied so far without doing harm to the doctrine of the Trinity, it is nevertheless a good illustration of a prince who willingly trades his rights and privileges with a pauper, and a pauper who becomes a prince. The prince didn't cease to be prince because he chose to be pauper-for-a-day. And Christ didn't cease to be Lord of all though He took on the form of a servant. But, to a point, He who knew no flesh took on flesh, and He who knew no sin took on sin, to become what we are so we could become what He is!

And here I was quibbling over communion!

When the service was over, I explained to the pastor what had brought me to the church, told him how I'd been convicted and said good-bye. I returned to my church as fast I could, where I apologized to the pastor for my attitude. My reaction had been sinful.

As a sinner, I desire to do what I want, when I want, how I want, for my own purposes. I want to do what I believe is my right, without consideration for what must be done or who will be hurt by exercising that right. As if there is no God who'll avenge me, I want to do what is right in my own eyes (Romans 12:19; Judges 17:6).

If Christ teaches anything, it is that the Christian life is one of self-denial, taking up my cross and following Him. That means dying to myself, what I want—my dreams, my hopes, my visions—and taking His as my own. That means delighting myself in God, taking joy in what He wants for me, even if and especially when it conflicts with what I want. As John Piper wrote in *Don't Waste Your Life!*, "God calls us to **pray and to think and to dream and to plan, not make much of us but to make much of Him."** This is where the rubber meets the road; it's one thing to talk about submission and quite another to do it, especially when the counsel I'm being given is not what I want to hear!

As Steven Curtis Chapman sings, "Fire up your engines, come on let's go, this is where the rubber meets the road. It's time to put in motion everything you know, this is where the rubber meets the road." I said I believed I had been foolish throughout my life, having made a host of bad decisions. I said I believe there is wisdom in the multitude of counselors. The rubber meets the road, however, when the counsel I am given goes against the grain and a decision must be made. Will I go my own way, as I have always done, or will I submit to those wiser than me?

Whether or not I am right is irrelevant. Christ is God. Christ is Right. Christ could have summoned the host of heaven instead of going to the cross. He didn't. He humbled Himself and was obedient even to the point of death. He let go of his "rights" and submitted to the will of the Father, though very God of very God. Such is the mystery, but He did it and so must I.

In another song Steven sings, "Now, let me say that I'm the kind of guy who wants to do it all myself, don't want to ask for help, don't like to stop for directions. . . .But in reality, I'm nothing on my own, it's by God's grace alone that I can make this confession. All that I am and all I'm hoping to be is all and only what He's given to me. . . . And I know this is how my life was meant to be, I was made for this dependency for the One who has created me. So I'll sing my declaration song, for the One I am depending on, and I hope you'll sing along. . . . This is my declaration of dependence, this is my declaration of my need, this is my declaration of dependence, on the One who gave His life to me." This is why the Apostle Paul said:

"Nor is He worshiped with men's hands, as though He needed anything, since He gives to all life, breath, and all things."
(Acts 17:25)

God made me to be dependent. I may refuse to admit it, but I am dependent on Him not only for salvation, but for life itself and the air I breathe! And, since I am dependent and God isn't in the private tutoring business, to whom shall I turn? (Compare Hebrews 1:1,2 with 2 Peter 1:20,21 and I Corinthians 12:12-31.) For this reason, God gave the church:

"And He Himself gave some to be apostles, some prophets, some evangelists, and some pastors and teachers, for the equipping of the saints for the work of ministry, for the edifying of the body of Christ, till we all come to the unity of the faith and of the knowledge of the Son of God, to a perfect man, to the measure of the stature of the fullness of Christ; that we should no longer be children, tossed to and fro and carried about with every wind of doctrine, by the trickery of men, in the cunning craftiness of deceitful plotting, but, speaking the truth in love, may grow up in all things into Him who is the head—Christ—from whom the whole body, joined and knit together by what every joint supplies, according to the effective working by which every

part does its share, causes growth of the body for the edifying of itself in love." (Ephesians 4:11-16)

***

I was on supervised probation for two years. As soon as my probation officer was able, he converted my case to unsupervised. By the grace of God, I was released from probation in 2001.

***

It seemed I had everything I needed. I had an incredible church home—the only real family I'd ever known. Yet, I couldn't escape the feeling that I was alone. I needed a helper. God made me for this purpose. He gave me hope I could one day be married. He did more to transform my life through watching the lives of the men and their families in that little church for less than a year than decades of deliverance services, countless fasts, and vain prayers had ever done. **I wanted it all.** I longed to be a husband and a father!

1. What does the author mean when he wrote, "in the grand scheme of things, I really didn't matter"?

   _____

   _____

   _____

2. If Christ is your savior, do you feel closer to or farther away from Him than when you first accepted Him? Why is this true?

   _____

   _____

   _____

3. Do you have a long history of making bad decisions?

_____

_____

_____

4. How can you be assured of making better decisions now and in the future?

_____

_____

_____

5. The author calls psychology "what is falsely called science." Do you agree or disagree with his assessment of it? Why or why not.

_____

_____

_____

6. This little church provided an incredible amount of financial assistance to the author. All they asked in return was that he (1) work and (2) regularly meet with them for financial accountability. Did they cross the line? Was this wrong?

_____

_____

_____

7. Is self-reliance sin?

_____

_____

_____

8. Should the author have been allowed to take communion before his public confession of faith?

_____

_____

_____

9. Based on Philippians 2, what does it mean to have "the mind of Christ"?

_____

_____

_____

10. How may our lives prove that we have the mind of Christ?

_____

_____

_____

11. Is trying to be independent a sin?

_____

_____

_____

12. List the reasons God has given the church.

_____

_____

_____

13. If God gave it, is attendance optional?

_____

_____

_____

NOTES

_____

_____

_____

_____

_____

_____

_____

_____

_____

_____

_____

_____

_____

_____

_____

_____

CHAPTER TWELVE:
MORE THAN REDEMPTION!

In 1979, Adams authored *A Theology for Christian Counseling: More Than Redemption*. Based on passages like John 10:10 and Romans 5:20, Adams wrote, "Salvation, that central concern of Protestant theology, is often too narrowly defined. It is thought to be 'being saved from the consequences of sin.' But God is doing much more. He is making new creatures. No matter what the problem is, no matter how greatly sin has abounded, the Christian counselor's stance is struck by the far-more-abounding nature of the grace of Jesus Christ in redemption."

***

Pastor Parnell urged me not to seek deliverance from remaining sin in the arms of a wife. I told him I was certain that deliverance wouldn't come through marriage alone, but that it cannot be denied that it is a means of grace, and I wanted to be married. During the interim, I needed work.

I started my first website development company out of my dorm room at Oklahoma State University, checkusout.net. My first official client was Timeless Texts, the publisher for Jay Adams! By God's grace, business grew and I decided to leave college rather than to continue to rack up even more student loans I may never be able to repay. With a felony conviction, I wasn't sure I'd have the opportunity to receive the full benefit of the public relations degree program in which I was enrolled anyway.

Throughout my life, mom and I still maintained a relationship and I frequently traveled to Dallas to visit her. Eventually, I moved the business to Dallas and managed to support myself.

Whenever the opportunity presented itself, I made myself available to date and meet many young women. I diligently sought a wife from the Reformed community. One woman claimed our date left her feeling as if she'd been in the presence of God! She obviously didn't know God or me very well. God's presence apparently left the building after she learned of my sinful past. I met several other women who were attracted to me, and one to whom I was attracted, but these relationships came to an end as soon as I mentioned my sin.

I finally decided to expand my search outside the Reformed community because it seemed none of the women I considered ideal were interested in someone with my past. I went on a date with a woman and her two children. We agreed that our relationship wasn't going much further, but not before she had introduced me to her best friend, Barbara.

Although I wasn't alive in the 1960s, even to this day, Barb reminds me of a hippy on steroids. She is full of laughter and has the most beautiful smile you have ever seen; she is the sweetest, kindest, most compassionate person you'll ever meet. Her whole life has been all about peace, love, and happiness! Toward that point, when I told her of my sin, her reaction was, "Is that all? I thought you were going to tell me something horrible; good lord, Chandler, we all sin!"

I still believe that God placed her in my life to teach me how to love others.

Barb has three children. Her oldest daughter, Danielle, died in an accident when she was 16. The next child, Shelly, was 17 when we met and on her way out of the house. She now lives in Arlington with her fiancé, Roscoe, and her one-year-old boy, Phenix. Brandon was eight. Today, Barb and I have been married almost eight years. Shelly is 26. Brandon is 17.

Brandon's "real" dad, Lee, died in 2008. I think I cried more than he did. After I called him out of school to tell him, he looked at me and said, "Well, I'm sad, and I'm surprised because I just saw him, but **you're my dad.**" At that moment, I imagined I heard the announcer for a commercial say, "Priceless. There are some things money can't buy." This was the "far-more-abounding nature of the grace of Jesus Christ in redemption" Jay was writing about. The thief came to steal, kill and destroy me, but Christ came that I would have life more abundantly—beyond anything I could ask or imagine! Where sin had abounded, grace does much more abound!

"Grace, grace, God's grace
Grace that is greater than all my sin"
Excerpted from Wonderful Grace of Jesus by Haldor Lillenas,
circa 1925

". . . as it is written:
'No eye has seen,
no ear has heard,
no mind has conceived
what God has prepared
for those who love him."
(I Corinthians 2:9)

1. By God's grace, the author experienced "more than redemption." Have you? Will you? How can you be certain?

_____

_____

_____

2. What do the following passages mean?

    a. In Romans 5:20, it is written, "where sin abounded, grace abounded much more."

_____

_____

_____

_____

    b. In John 10:10, it is written, "The thief came to steal, kill, and destroy, but Christ came that you might have life, and that more abundantly."

_____

_____

_____

_____

    c. In Jeremiah 29:11, it is written, "For I know the thoughts that I think toward you, says the LORD, thoughts of peace and not of evil, to give you a future and a hope."

_____

_____

_____

_____

3. What is hope?

_____

_____

_____

4. Have you lost hope?

    _____

    _____

    _____

    _____

5. In whom should you place your hope?

    _____

    _____

    _____

    _____

6. In the case of the author, God converted a user and abuser of everyone and everything into a husband, father, and servant of the gospel. Practically speaking, **what would this hope mean for you?**

    _____

    _____

    _____

    _____

NOTES

_____

_____

_____

_____

CHAPTER THIRTEEN:
A CHANGE GONNA COME

In the movie *8 Mile*, Eminem plays "Rabbit," a young man who has wrestled his whole life with demons: a neglectful, alcoholic, whoring mother; her many boyfriends; poverty; having to be a parent to his younger sister; and the stigma of being white and an aspiring rapper. The way to the top, the way to gain street "cred," was for him to "battle" other rappers to see who was better at putting the other down. In his finest moment, Rabbit "flipped the script" on his opponent. He began his battle by saying everything that anyone could possibly say against him. In so doing, he left his accuser speechless. Of course, that's Hollywood.

In real life, this is the hardest chapter for me to write. Given the nature of my crimes, I know I can't finish this book without answering the question: "Do you still struggle with the temptation that led you to prison?"

I long for the day when I can answer that question, "No."

Wait a minute, you exclaim, I thought you said you had been converted! I thought your sin was gone. I thought you "turned from idols to serve God." All true. Yet I sin.

I have heard of people who were, for a lack of a better term, what I would call "zapped." That is, I have heard of others who have struggled with some sexual sin say that God completely removed their desire to commit *that* sin from the moment they became Christians. I know of a prominent worship leader who claims this happened to him. He was a practicing homosexual for many years, but he has been a faithful husband for many more and is the father of ten children! Not me. I still struggle.

I can tell you that the pattern of behavior the state used to convict me with is broken. Forever. **I can tell you that then my heart was inclined to evil and all I knew was sin; today my heart is inclined toward righteousness and now I know what it is to choose not to sin from a grateful heart.** And, thirteen years later, I still surround myself with godly men from whom I seek counsel and accountability. I always have access to the counsel of four or five godly men on speed dial or by e-mail.

I can also tell you that, by God's grace, He has made me into a husband and a father. He has allowed me to have a real impact in the lives of other young men. Groaning with all of creation for the day of my final redemption from sin—glorification, when I'll put off corruptibility and put on incorruptibly, put off mortality and put on immortality—I remain hopeful. And I know from these first fruits that this isn't a hope that has or ever will disappoint.

In fact, I was even asked by my son's school to teach high-school chapel. I sought counsel from my pastor as to whether or not he thought it would be wise to do so and, if so, whether or not I must confess my sins to them before accepting. Given the grace I'd received and the environment—that it would only be for one hour each week and that I would always be supervised with other teachers in the room—he saw no reason for me to volunteer my past unless I was asked. I taught that chapel for a full school year.

I have already stated that what I learned about the result of true, saving faith from Morey's book, *Studies in the Atonement*, is that the faith that saves is also the faith that changes lives. Whom the Son sets free is free indeed! Paul stated it best:

"How are we who are dead to sin to continue therein? God forbid!" (Romans 6:1).

Christ Himself learned obedience through being tested (Hebrews 5:8). **Whereas Christ never failed a test, I have.** The answer is in Paul's question, ""How are we who are dead to sin to *continue* therein?" (emphasis added). I can tell you that I have not continued in *that* sin. If I said I do not sin, I'd be a liar (I John 1:8). The good news of the gospel is that, when I sin, I have the Advocate, Jesus Christ the righteous, with my Father (I John 1:9).

> *"For a righteous man may fall seven times and rise again,*
> *but the wicked shall fall by calamity" Proverbs 24:16*

In the song "We Fall Down," Bob Carlisle tells the story of a poor village boy who frequently passed a monastery's high cathedral wall; it made his life seem meaningless and small. Every day as he passed, he'd wonder what it would be like to be "warm, well fed, and at peace, to shut the world away." One day, a priest ventured beyond the iron gate. In awe of this godly man, the boy asked him what his life was like. With age-old wisdom, the priest replied, "We fall down; we get up. We fall down; we get up. We fall down; we get up. And **the saints are just the sinners who fall down . . . and get up."**

Perhaps one of my greatest present struggles is with envy. I know men whose worst, visible sin may have been stealing cookies from the cookie jar. They began in grace, were raised in Christian homes, converted at a young age, have prospered as only the righteous can do. They are happily married and the best of husbands and fathers. They have been at the work of purifying their souls in obeying the truth far longer than I. In God's providence, it's nearly all they've ever known. And the same will probably be true for their children.

And sometimes I shake my fist toward the sky and ask, "Why them and not me, God?"

Then I remember the words of Peter about "what the angels have longed to see" and I bow my head in awe. For I both know and have experienced the love and the grace of God first-hand! I remember my sin with shame, yet I know that God has allowed me the privilege of knowing Him in a way that some may never know. For Christ said, "Those who have been forgiven much, love much" (Luke 7:36-50).

As John Piper wrote in *Don't Waste Your Life*, "Love has to do with showing a dying soul the life-giving beauty of the glory of God, especially His grace." Every day, His mercies are new every morning, and that love compels me! And Piper continues, "If it is true, as the Psalmist says to God, 'In Your presence there is fullness of joy; at your right hand are pleasures evermore,' (Psalm 16:11), then what must love do? It must rescue us from our addiction to self and bring us, changed, into the presence of God."

I would end that string of pearls with an exclamation point: What must love do? . . . It must rescue me from my addiction to self and bring me into the presence of God! Love and gratitude compel me to keep pressing on, to keep taking my teaspoon to that mountain of sin. Love for God, stemming from a real knowledge of my sin and the depth of His love for me anyway, is what continues to transform my life from a vessel of dishonor into a trophy of His grace!

***

Not too long ago, I was able to have lunch with Skip Ryan, chancellor and professor of practical theology at Redeemer Theological Seminary, Dallas, Texas.

He said he'd been thinking a lot about sanctification recently and had been pondering what the mechanism is that makes people want to turn from sin to serve God. He asked me what I thought.

I told him that I recently saw Kirk Cameron on television. When asked why he became a Christian, Kirk said he came to a place in his life where he had everything he wanted but no one to whom he felt thankful. When he heard the Gospel, he realized God was the source of all his success, and from that point on he just wanted to live his life in a way that said, "Thank you."

I told Skip I felt like that is what does it for me: gratitude. As I learn more and more about my sin and the grace of God despite it, I am overwhelmed with gratitude for that grace, and I just want to live my life in a way that says, "Thank you." An attitude of gratitude becomes my motivation for continued growth.

***

The difference between then and now is that I win more than I lose. Enslaved to sin, all I knew was sin. Now a slave to righteousness, I know what it is not to sin. I "continue" not in sin but in righteousness. I remain confident and hopeful there will come a day, perhaps even in this lifetime, when I can honestly say that I no longer struggle with *that* sin either in my heart or in practice.

Until then, I surround myself with the means of grace: the Word, prayer, the sacraments, the Church, marriage, and more. I continue to do so even when, I confess to my shame, I sometimes fall or sometimes desire to do otherwise. I fall but I get back up. I groan. I long. I wait.

This hope won't disappoint. For he who has begun this work in me will be faithful to complete it (Phil 1:6). Until then, I must choose whom I will worship, moment by moment, day by day.

"To all the travelers
Pilgrims longing for a home
From one who walks with you
On this journey called life's road
It is a long and winding road
From one who's seen the view
And dreamt of staying on the mountains high

And one who's cried like you
Wanting so much to lay down and die
I offer this, we must remember this
"We are not home yet. . . .

"I know there'll be a moment
I know there'll be a place
Where we will see our Savior
And fall in His embrace
So let us not grow weary
Or too content to stay
'Cause we are not home yet
We are not home yet...
Keep on looking ahead
Let you heart not forget
We are not home yet"

Excerpted from "Not Home Yet" by Steven Curtis Chapman.

1. What's the difference between committing a sin and "habitual sin"?

_____

_____

_____

2. Are both types of sin present in the life of a Christian?

_____

_____

_____

3. What's the difference between the sinner and the saint?

_____

_____

_____

4. Have you been forgiven much?

_____

_____

_____

5. If you've been forgiven, what must be your response to sinners and to other Christians struggling with sin?

_____

_____

_____

NOTES

_____

_____

_____

_____

_____

_____

_____

_____

_____

_____

CHAPTER FOURTEEN:
MADE FOR WORSHIPPING

"When I'm playing with my children
As they're running off to school
When I kiss my wife good morning
Just to say I still love you
When I'm feeling loved and happy
When I'm feeling all alone
When I'm failing to remember
All the love that's been shown
Every beat of my heart is another
new place to start to know.

"This is a moment made for worshiping
'Cause this is a moment I'm alive
This is a moment I was made to sing
A song of living sacrifice
For every moment that I live and breathe
This is a moment made for worshipping"

Excerpted from "Moment Made for Worshipping"
by Steven Curtis Chapman.

In *Confessions*, Saint Augustine wrote, "You have made us for Yourself and restless is our heart until it comes to rest in You." Toby Mac raps about this fact:

> *"I was made to love You*
> *I was made to find You*
> *I was made just for You*
> *Made to adore You*
> *I was made to love and be loved by You*
> *You were here before me*
> *You were waiting on me*
> *And You said You'd keep me never would You leave me*
> *I was made to love*
> *And be loved by You."*

Excerpted from "Made to Love" by TobyMac.

Restless had been my heart prior to my conversion. Restless is my heart after my conversion. The aim of my restlessness is decidedly different. I was restless to get what I wanted, regardless of how great my sin or who I used and abused. Today, I am restless to be free of this sin forever.

The only helpful observation I ever gained from years of reading humanistic, self-help, and secular psychology texts came from William Glasser. In *Control Theory*, Glasser wrote that I am born into this world with basic needs. He said that I am born with a blank slate, an empty photo album, if you will. He said the way I learn what I want is that, whenever I first experience something that fills a particular need, I take a picture of it and place it in my mental photo album. Once the picture is in my album, I will go back to it over and over again to satisfy that need until something comes along that satisfies it even more. When something does satisfy a need more, then I throw out the old picture and replace it with whatever satisfies me more. Glasser also commented that this is why it is often difficult if not impossible for people with sexual problems to change. In particular, the pictures I take that satisfy sexual needs are so a part of me that few things, if any, will come along that will be able to satisfy me more.

Glasser, of course, wasn't a Christian when he wrote this book. Had he been a Christian, he would have known that I am not born *tabula rasa*—with a blank slate, as he suggests. I am born with a nature that is already inclined to the worst evils. Some just manifest this nature more than others. And, of course, with regard to change, Glasser knew nothing of the gospel.

For the last several years, at the bottom of every e-mail I send, has been the following quote from C.S. Lewis:

". . . if we consider the unblushing promises of reward and the staggering nature of the rewards promised in the Gospels, it would seem that Our Lord finds our desires not too strong, but too weak. We are half-hearted creatures, fooling about with drink and sex and ambition when infinite joy is offered us, like an ignorant child who wants to go on making mud pies in a slum because he cannot imagine what is meant by the offer of a holiday at the sea. We are far too easily pleased." (C.S. Lewis, *The Weight of Glory*)

Lewis got it right! **I need to see my sin for what it is: a sinful exchange of truth, beauty, and a life of joy for the lies offered by fleeting passions!** If my life is not to be wasted, it must be about seeing sin as God sees it, replacing sinful with righteous patterns of behavior, and finding my true joy in what pleases and honors God.

Again from *Don't Waste Your Life*, **Piper wrote, "The opposite of wasting your life is living life by a single God-exalting, soul-satisfying passion."** That passion is to display knowing Christ in the way that we live as supremely valuable above anyone and anything else. As it is written: "You are worthy, O Lord, to receive glory and honor and power; for You created all things, And by Your will they exist and were created." (Revelations 4:11)

In Romans 1, Paul wrote that the wrath of God is revealed against me because I (1) suppress the truth, (2) live with ingratitude as if God isn't our creator, (3) exchange His immortal glory for that which is corruptible, (4) exchange His truth for a lie, and (5) worship the creation instead of the Creator.

Bob Dylan sang about it, "You may be [whatever] but you're gonna have to serve somebody." In "Moment Made for Worshipping," Steven Curtis Chapman declared that every moment is a moment made for worshipping; from the seemingly mundane to the majestic, worship is all of life! It is said that "we live our life Coram Deo," before God.

I was made to worship. It shows.

Until the day I was converted, I worshipped Chandler, all the time. I did what I wanted, when I wanted, how I wanted. I used and abused everyone and everything to my own ends, for my own sinful pleasure. I was not new to worshipping; I was new to worshipping God.

Quoting some local poets, which then became part of Scripture, Paul said ". . . in Him we live, and move, and have our being" (Acts 17:28). Every day I realize it more. Worship isn't just what I do on Sunday or at some other service. Worship is what I do during every moment of my life. Either I am worshipping self or I am worshipping God.

I live my life moment by moment for the here and now, but Christ lived his life always connected to the transcendent God, the God who exists everywhere, all times, in all places. This is why Christ commanded me to seek first the kingdom, to set my mind on things above and not on things below. I am to be ever-conscious of God's presence with me, ever mindful that my every thought, word, and deed is ever before my God.

I've learned that everything begins with repentance, renewing my mind by the Word of God, being transformed by it and not conformed to the world around me, replacing sinful with righteous behaviors.

Nowhere has my own sinful refusal to recognize that all of life is worship been more apparent than on my bed at night. Fleeting thoughts become fantasies, fantasy becomes masturbation, and sin begets sin. Change began when I realized that worship is as much what I do on my bed as on Sunday before the congregation. Every moment is a moment made for worshipping. Either I am going to live my life worshipping my Creator—proving in my own thoughts, words, and deeds that He is God and that He is worthy of my sacrifice and praise—or I am going to worship self—proving in my thoughts, words, and deeds that what I want is more important than what He's commanded.

As I consider my ongoing struggle with sin, it's also important to remember that God is sovereign. His sovereignty isn't checked at the door when temptation and sin enter my life. Instead of living as if there is no God, I need to view my temptation in the light of this truth. God is sovereign. If I did not have this struggle, would I still remember Him? Would I worship Him without a visible need? If I focus only on the struggle, only on the sin, I am guilty of acting as if He's not there with me. Instead, **if I am tempted twelve times in a day, I need to view each one as being a Call to Worship from the God who made me, loved me, and gave Himself for me!** This is life. Life is worship.

***

I was recently asked to become a "pod pastor" to men on death row. The Alan Polunsky death row unit is divided into eight "pods" (sections) with 84 men on each pod. Six pods are for strictly "death row" inmates; two pods are for inmates in Administrative Segregation, those who are generally considered the most violent offenders. There is one man to each 6-foot by 10-foot cell. The men are on 23-hour lockdown; they are allowed one hour of recreation time, one at a time, each day. The Polunsky facility houses just under 3,000, and the chaplains just don't have enough time to see all the men. The chaplain over death row invited me to care for one of the pods by visiting the men on a regular basis.

One of the young men I met—I am guessing he is between 18 and 22—had been sentenced to and just recently began serving two life sentences. Initially, thinking I was part of the official chaplain's office, he refused to speak with me. Once he learned I had driven more than 200 miles just to visit the men on that pod, he opened up. He told me he had been reading a book that said we were called to be slaves to God on this earth, that God has a way He wants us to live, things He wants us to do. And the young man said he just wasn't "down for that."

I said, "Look, you and I were made to worship. We're going to worship something or someone. The only question is whom or what. I worshipped myself. I was all about that. I did what I wanted, when I wanted, how I wanted, and I didn't care who got hurt. I used and abused everything and everyone to get what I wanted. I went to prison. Now, if you're honest, you've done the same thing. You worshipped yourself and look where it got you. You're in here. I'm out here. We were made to worship. All I can tell you is that my life is better worshipping God than worshipping myself."

**

In the DVD sermon by the same name as the Piper book, *Don't Waste Your Life*, Piper quotes Philippians 3:7—"But what things were gain to me, these I have counted loss for Christ," and then asks, "How do you make it plain to all who are watching that Christ is your treasure?" Piper says that Paul displayed the supreme worth of Christ in the way that he counted everything else loss, even his very life, to gain more of Christ. He continues by saying that we also should display the infinite value we place on Christ in the way that we live. And to illustrate he offers the following examples:

- Friends, family, even enemies, are in your life so that it will be plain in the way that you love them that Christ first loved you!

- Money is entrusted to you so that you make it plain in the way you live and give to others that money is not your treasure, Christ is.

- Food is yours to eat so that you make it plain in the way you eat that food is not your treasure, Christ is!

- A home, cars, computers, cell phones, and all else is entrusted to you so that it will be plain in the way that you use these that they are not your treasure, Christ is!

- Christ's infinite value is displayed when seeing Him means more to you than everything and everyone you will leave behind. If death is to be gain, Christ must be more precious to you than life and everything in it.

What does it mean when I say that life is worship? It means that in everything I think, say and do, I am either treasuring Christ or sin. I am either evidencing by my actions that Christ is more valuable to me than my sin or, God forbid, that my sin is of greater worth than Christ.

While writing this book, my weight peaked at over 380 pounds. My son had a weight problem also. One day, after a few of his own failed diet attempts, my son came up to me and said, "This time it's going to work, dad, because this time I've asked God to help me and I know He will." Within six months, he lost 50 pounds!

Although I saw clearly that every moment of my life was made for worship, the words of my son struck right to the core. As Piper had said, "Food is yours to eat so that you make it plain in the way you eat that food is not your treasure, Christ is!" I was faced with a choice. Continue worshipping myself and what I wanted, which was the best-tasting, worst possible food for me, or begin to eat the way God would have me and to shed the pounds.

For me, making the right choices about what to eat and when is worship. Like my son, I too had been dieting off and on but I have only been truly persistent and consistent in my effort to lose weight since my son came to me that day. I recently weighed in at 362. I am committed to taking the weight off slowly. No fad diet. As a nutritionist at the Cooper Clinic I once heard speak said, "Dieting is just simple math: you have to get rid of more than you're taking in."

One night the chaplain from the prison in which I minister and I went out for dinner. I could choose grilled catfish or a loaded, baked potato stuffed with barbecue, the size of Rhode Island. Then I chose the grilled catfish and a salad. **I will fall down but I'll get back up again (John 6:44).**

This is my pedigree: God chose me not because I was the smartest but because I am the most foolish, the weakest, the lowest, the most despised. As Paul wrote:

"For you see your calling, brethren, that not many wise accord-ing to the flesh, not many mighty, not many noble, are called. But God has chosen the foolish things of the world to put to shame the wise, and God has chosen the weak things of the world to put to shame the things which are mighty; and the base things of the world and the things which are despised God has chosen, and the things which are not, to bring to nothing the things that are, that no flesh should glory in His presence. But of Him you are in Christ Jesus, who became for us wisdom from God—and righteousness and sanctification and redemption—that, as it is written, "He who glories, let him glory in the LORD." (I Corinthians 1:26-31)

After reading *Don't Waste Your Life* by—you guessed it, John Piper, Steven Curtis Chapman asks in a song he wrote:

". . .how can I kneel here
And think of the cross
The thorns and the whip
and the nails and the spear
The infinite cost
To purchase my pardon
And bear all my shame
To think I have anything worth boasting in
Except for Your name
Cause I am a sinner
And You are the Savior and. . .

"I want to make much of You, Jesus
I want to make much of Your love
I want to live today to give You the praise
That You alone are so worthy of
I want to make much of Your mercy
I want to make much of Your cross
I give You my life
Take it and let it be used
To make much of You."

Excerpted from "Much of You" by Steven Curtis Chapman.

As I quoted earlier, Piper wrote in *Don't Waste Your Life*, "God calls us to pray and to think and to dream and to plan, not to be made much of, but to make much of Him." To worship self and Satan is to consistently choose to live as if there is no God, to do what I want, when I want, how I want, based on whatever is right to me; to worship God is to begin consciously making choices that make it plain that He is my greatest treasure, denying my own desires, replacing them with Him.

1. What did Augustine mean when he wrote, "You have made us for Yourself and restless is our heart until it comes to rest in you. . ."?

   _____

   _____

   _____

2. According to Glasser, we are born with a blank slate. Is this true or false?

   _____

   _____

   _____

3. Are you able to recognize some of the times when you have been guilty of exchanging the truth for a lie, worshipping the creature instead of the Creator?

   _____

   _____

   _____

4. Is all of life really worship?

_____

_____

_____

5. How do we evidence what or whom we're worshipping?

_____

_____

_____

6. What does it mean to live "connected to the transcendent"?

_____

_____

_____

7. Will God complete the work He's started in you?

_____

_____

_____

8. Have you been changed behind bars? In what way?

_____

_____

_____

CONCLUSION

So, what was missing from the prayer I prayed with that pastor? It was my own ignorance as to the extent of my sin's depravity and my own realization that I was unable to save myself. To the first I was simply blinded and now, absent Divine intervention, I believe the latter may only be learned after years of experience. (And even that will take a miracle!) At the time, I had neither spiritual insight nor very much of a history. But I have written enough about me. Let's talk about you.

You've been blaming the hypocrites for your refusal to repent. Honestly, it's just that you've enjoyed—perhaps even still enjoy, doing what you want, when you want, how you want. Hey, let's be real, there really is pleasure in sin for a season! But look where it has led you. Much of your life has been wasted. Bridges have been burned. Be grateful you're not dead yet. Repent. Believe on the Lord Jesus and be saved!

And to you hypocrites! "Well did Isaiah prophesy about you, saying: 'These people draw near to me with their mouth, and honor me with their lips, but their heart is far from me . . . .'" (Matthew 15:7-9). I know you well because that passage described me. And sometimes still does. But if you've really come to know Christ, then the change should be evident. You should win more than you lose. Your life should show forth that you treasure Christ above everything and everyone else. Unless you repent and place your trust in Christ, you will be like one of those to whom Christ says, "I never knew you; depart from me, you who practice lawlessness!"

But to you who are weary and worn, Christ bids you come: "Come to Me, all you who labor and are heavy laden, and I will give you rest. Take My yoke upon you and learn from Me, for I am gentle and lowly in heart, and you will find rest for your souls. For My yoke is easy and My burden is light." (Matthew 11:28-30) You are at your lowest point? Then you are at the best point for Christ to save you! Have you been a fool? Are you weak? You have done the worst of all? Do you think yourself unworthy? Read God's Word to you:

He who humbles himself will be exalted; God has chosen to save the foolish, the weak, the worst of the worst, so that you can't take any of the credit. He is sure to get the most glory because of the greatness of your sin. And because of His salvation, you'll love and serve Him in a way that others cannot, who foolishly believe they have less to forgive. (Luke 18:14; I Corinthians 1:26-31; Luke 7:47)

The purpose of this book was to demonstrate that a real decision to accept Christ must occur in the historical context of having learned (1) the extent of our sinful depravity, (2) that we are unable to save ourselves, and (3) that we are without hope for salvation apart from Christ and so we (4) rest our faith and trust in Christ. The salvation experience of everyone will not unfold the same in history; the times and circumstances will be different. But man, sin, God and the requirements of salvation are the same; hence, redemptive history should lead all Christians to confess at least the following:

- We are born in sin; every thought and intent of our heart is only evil, continually. (This is big! Make sure you get it.)

- We have all been sentenced to die for our sin and His wrath abides on us.

- We are without hope to save ourselves; there is no other way we may be saved. (This is even bigger!)

- God sent His son to die for our sins.

- His death is completely sufficient to save us.

- We can neither add to nor take anything away from His salvation. (This is—well, okay, how can it keep getting bigger, but it's at least as important as the last—so this is bigger too!)

- Our lives will show that we are saved by the way we—progressively more and more, display the supreme worth and infinite value of Christ over everything and everyone else.

Believe me when I tell you that the bulleted list above is not unique to one denomination or another. This is the gospel; this is the faith that was once for all delivered to the saints (Jude 3). I can say with Paul that there will come a day when God will judge the secrets of men according to "my gospel." (Romans 2:16)

Do you think you've sinned too greatly? Harmed too many people? Burned too many bridges? So that God must be unwilling or unable to save you? The good news of the gospel is that you are EXACTLY the person He desires to save! Christ said He came to save the sick—those who realize their sinful condition, feel and believe their need of the Great Physician. Moses, Paul, and David were all murderers! David was an adulterer as well. Paul claimed to be "the worst" or "chief of sinners." You are EXACTLY the one God has chosen!

"For . . . not many wise according to the flesh, not many mighty, not many noble, are called. But God has chosen the foolish things of the world to put to shame the wise, and God has chosen the weak things of the world to put to shame the things which are mighty; and the base things of the world and the things which are despised God has chosen, and the things which

are not, to bring to nothing the things that are, that no flesh should glory in His presence. But of Him you are in Christ Jesus, who became for us wisdom from God—and righteousness and sanctification and redemption—that, as it is written, 'He who glories, let him glory in the LORD.'" (I Corinthians 1:26-31)

Sometimes I think I may have inherited my mom's so-called schizophrenia because I sometimes imagine myself having a conversation with God. It goes like this:

> I ask, "Why would You choose me? What have I ever done to deserve Your grace?"
>
> To which He replies, "Nothing."
>
> Still unsure, to be certain I heard Him correctly, hesitantly I ask, "Nothing?"
>
> And definitively He answers, "Exactly."
>
> Then He explains, "When I save the worst of sinners, the world stops and listens and the angels look on in wonder! And you who have been forgiven much will love and serve me more than those who did not feel their need of me as strongly."

Have you come to see yourself as a sinner in need of a savior? Indeed, not just a sinner, but the worst of sinners? Do you value the sacrifice Christ made on your behalf—one that was not mandatory, but certainly was necessary if you were to be saved? Do you see the greatness of your sin in the price that it cost—the death of Christ upon the cross? Are you experiencing the power of the resurrection in your life—the power that is about more than just being spared the punishment of your sin? Have you really been set free from sin? Do you win more than you lose?

If you're waiting for me to lead you in a prayer, you'll be waiting a long time! The gospel doesn't begin with an enchantment. It begins with a change of mind—you admit you're a sinner, that you're unable to save yourself, and that you deserve nothing; it results in a change of direction—you stop trusting in yourself, trying to save yourself, and you submit to the Lord's will and His means of grace for your life (Bible study, prayer, church fellowship, accountability and discipline, baptism and communion). It's a reorientation of one's life from the sinful self to the sinless Savior. There aren't any words or any magic potions that will do it for you. When it happens, how it happens, has nothing to do with you. It has everything to do with Him. Your only hope is to cry out to God for mercy. The good news is that when you do He is there.

But redemption is about more than being spared the Divine sentence; it is about more than just that I was saved from the penalty of sin and the flames of hell. The power of the gospel is in the death and resurrection of Christ to transform my life from the worst of sinners into the least of saints! Christ was raised so that I who had been an abuser would one day be a husband, father, high-school chapel teacher, and trusted mentor! For this purpose God chose me, the Spirit called me, Christ atoned for me, the Spirit keeps me, and I will one day be with Him in glory!

"For I through the law died to the law that I might live to God. I have been crucified with Christ; it is no longer I who live, but Christ lives in me; and the life which I now live in the flesh I live by faith in the Son of God, who loved me and gave Himself for me." (Galatians 2:19-20)

This is a story about more than just one who was CHANGED BEHIND BARS; it's a story about an abuser who became a husband, father, author and evangelist! Where are you on the road to redemption? Are you still under the tutor of the law? How long must you be shown your sinfulness and inability to change before you finally humble yourself before God and confess your sins?

Believe the gospel and you will be saved!

I know it sounds crazy to end on this note but are you schizophrenic too? Can you hear God singing over you? You should.

"The Lord our God; He is with you.
He is mighty to save.
The Lord our God; He is with you.
He is mighty to save.
If you could only hear His voice,
You would hear the Lord rejoice,
rejoicing over you, rejoicing over you,
rejoicing over you, with singing."

--From a song based on Zephaniah 3:17, author unknown

NOTES

_____

_____

_____

_____

_____

_____

_____

_____

_____

_____

_____

APPENDIX A: BOOK BLOG

While I was editing this book, I found many things I'd written that I regard as important but that nevertheless seemed to interrupt the flow of the book. With the modern advent of blogs, I thought it would be cool to create a sort of blog for this book. Since most blogs tend to be a series of unrelated topics that happen to be on the author's mind at any given moment, and since most people are used to following one or more of them anyway, this seems like a perfect fit. And, hey, if you find out you like the way I think, why not follow my real blog at www.ChangedBehindBars.com!

The Process of Salvation

(Cut from the INTRODUCTION)

Today, I understand the Scripture to teach that salvation is more a process and less an event. As a Christian:

- I have been JUSTIFIED—saved from the *penalty* of sin.

- I am being SANCTIFIED—saved from the *power* of sin.

- I will be GLORIFIED—saved from the *presence* of sin.

By His electing grace, I was justified—declared righteous before God on the basis of Christ's work, through faith alone—and even my very faith was a gift!

"Therefore, my beloved, as you have always obeyed, not as in my presence only, but now much more in my absence, work out your own salvation with fear and trembling; for it is God who works in you both to will and to do for His good pleasure."
(Philippians 2:12-13.)

After I was saved from the penalty of sin—justified and, thus, declared righteous, the process of salvation continues while I am being sanctified—set apart for God's use. Sanctification may be said to be a cooperative effort; by His grace, "I die daily". As Piper wrote in *Don't Waste Your Life*, "God calls us to pray and to think and to dream and to plan, not to be made much of, but to make much of Him." Dying daily, I begin to learn how to pray and think and dream and plan so as to glorify Him, not to make much of me. As I purify my soul in obeying the truth, which I can only do by His grace, God works His will and the ability to do His will in my life more and more.

"...we ourselves groan within ourselves, eagerly waiting for the adoption, the redemption of our body." (Romans 8:23)

Then, finally, will come the day I will be glorified. I will put off what is corruptible and put on what is incorruptible! I will put off what perishes and put on what will never perish! Finally, I will sing in the words of the old spiritual, "Free at last, free at last, thank God Almighty, I am free at last!" This is the process of salvation, but even it seems to progress in stages, so that the process itself becomes more a marathon and less of a sprint.

Left to Myself

(Cut from the end of Chapter Two: BORN IN SIN)

"Train up a child in the way he should go, And when he is old he will not depart from it." (Proverbs 22:6)

The passage above is often used to encourage parents to train up their children in the way of the Lord while they are young. According to the interpretation of some, if we raise our children to follow Christ, they will remain faithful and grow up to live as Christians.

In *Christian Living in the Home*, Jay Adams writes that this verse actually refers to children who are left to raise themselves. He says that the verse is really more of a warning than it is meant to provide any encouragement. In my case, the passage would more accurately be understood that, left to raise myself, it was going to be harder—if not impossible—for me to change as I grew older. I would continue to rebel. I would do whatever was right in my own eyes because that would be all I knew. With dad dead, mom "nuts," no relationship with God, or even positive role models, I was certainly left to myself.

Does Total Depravity Mean I Am As Bad As I Can Be Always?

(Cut from the end of Chapter Two: BORN IN SIN)

Neither the doctrine of original sin, nor even of the total depravity of man, state that I am as evil as I could be all the time or that I never do anything some might call "good." It simply states that I am born with a nature enslaved to sin and, apart from Divine intervention, I will choose sin every time. As we will see from Scripture and my own life later, according to His good pleasure, God restrains and allows goodness and wickedness.

That is not to say God is the author of sin. When I sin, He does not drag me kicking and screaming.

"Let no one say when he is tempted, 'I am tempted by God'; for God cannot be tempted by evil, nor does He Himself tempt anyone. But each one is tempted when he is drawn away by his own desires and enticed." (James 1:13,14).

When I am tempted, I freely sin. It is my nature to do so. Left to myself, I do so unreservedly. But God is often pleased to enable me to act righteously (if only for a moment, for His purposes) or to allow sin to reign. I confess it's a mystery.

"The secret things belong to the LORD our God, but those things which are revealed belong to us and to our children forever, that we may do all the words of this law." (Deuteronomy 29:29)

Regarding I Corinthians 10:13

(Cut from the end of Chapter Nine: NO SPECIAL CASES)

Darwin Jordan, the pastor of the church I attend now, alluded in a recent sermon series on this passage that many have cited this verse to provide a false sense of comfort to those who struggle with habitual sin. "It's okay," one might say, "We all sin." Adams wasn't saying that. Jay's emphasis is that, just as assuredly as all have sinned and that God has delivered them, He was and is able to deliver me. Hence, there was and is no excuse for me to continue in sin. Darwin said that the text was a warning that, if I continue to play with fire, just as God had judged the children of Israel "and in one day twenty-three thousand fell," I will get burned.

The Condition of Man

(Cut from the Conclusion)

It has been said...

Before the fall man was able not to sin.

After the fall man is not able not to sin.

After Christ man is once more able not to sin.

In Heaven man will not be able to sin.

A Theological, Chronological Ordering of My Salvation

(Cut from the Conclusion)

As Morey wrote in *Studies in the Atonement*, ". . . no one theologian can claim that his order is 'logical' as opposed to the 'illogical' arrangement of another," for all are "logical as far as form is concerned". Morey argued that perhaps a theological arrangement might be best that sees each of the elements "related to and dependent upon the nucleus," which is union with Christ. I have arranged the stages of my salvation in a chronological order in this book.

In the end, having attempted to arrange the order of my own salvation experience chronologically, I understand Morey's argument more than ever. I shudder when I think about the nature and implications of suggesting one element occurs before or after another. At best, failing to understand the order properly distorts the true order of salvation when, in time and space, an element may have occurred at once, over time, or still be awaiting completion. At worst, it results in heresy and—were it possible—it may even deceive the elect.

Although the exact order of all the elements may not be certain, the arrangement of two elements is absolutely certain: regeneration precedes faith; I am saved and therefore I believe. If I have demonstrated anything in this text, I pray I have made the case that regeneration had to precede faith because I was born dead in sin, and so were you. The knowledge that I am a sinner must of necessity come before I may know my need for a savior; for they that believe themselves to be whole see no need of a physician (Matthew 9:12).

In chronological order, then, following is the history of my redemption:

God **PREDESTINED** me before the foundation of the world, before I had done any good or evil.[6] Nevertheless, I was born **TOTALLY DEPRAVED** in sin, such that the thoughts and intents of my heart were only wicked, continually. After saying that "prayer" as a teenager, I entered the school of hard knocks and was **TUTORED BY THE LAW** until I would come to Christ years later (Galatians 3:24). Again, the law teaches me that I am powerless over my sin and unable to save myself.

As I read *Studies in the Atonement*, God **CALLED** me through the preaching of the gospel. The Spirit **REGENERATED** me: He took out my heart of stone and gave me a heart of flesh, granting me wisdom (eyes to see) and the revelation of the knowledge that is found in Christ (ears to hear).

---

6   I will spare you the debate as to whether or not He made the choice before or after the fall [supra- or infra-lapsarianism, respectively.

Having regenerated and called me, **FAITH WAS GIFTED IN MY HEART** by the Holy Spirit. I **REPENTED**, which began with an acknowledgement that I was a sinner in need of a savior and began to turn from sin to serve Him. Believing, I was **CONVERTED** and translated out of the kingdom of darkness into His kingdom of light!

Upon belief and repentance, I was placed in **UNION WITH CHRIST**. In Christ, His **SACRIFICE** resulted in my **REDEMPTION**, Christ having paid the penalty for my sin; **PROPITIATION**, God's removal of His wrath from my sin because of the death of Christ on the cross; **RECONCILIATION**, which resulted in peace between God and me; and **EXPIATION**, God removing my sin and guilt from before Him. As such, I was **JUSTIFIED**, declared and made righteous before Him.

Upon which declaration, I was **ADOPTED**, grafted into the family of God. I am being **SANCTIFIED**, which means I am learning how to treasure Christ above all else in heart and in practice, more and more, every day, in every way, as I work at the purification of my soul in obedience to the truth.

The Spirit **PRESERVES** me, keeping me in the faith until the end, never leaving me in sin without effectually calling me back. As such, I **PERSEVERE**, for it is He who works in me both the will and the ability to do of His good pleasure. Therefore, I have complete **ASSURANCE** that He who began this work in me will keep me until the day of Christ's return.

I shall be **GLORIFIED** in heaven when I receive the **CROWN OF LIFE** from the one who gave His life for me. And so, I will lay my crown at His feet, and worship and serve forever the One who became wisdom from God for me, righteousness, sanctification and redemption, and still managed to find it in His heart to say, "Well done, thou good and faithful servant," when the best I contributed was the worst of my sin.

Illustrating the Process of Salvation with the Beatitudes

(Cut from the end of the Epilogue)

I have also seen the Beatitudes used to illustrate the progression of the Christian life.

Beatitude	Order of Salvation
Poor in spirit	We realize our depravity
Mourning	We despair over sin
Meek	We walk humbly before our God
Hunger and thirst after righteousness	We study His Word and fellowship
Merciful	We forgive as we have been forgiven
Pure in heart	We strive to live holy; we guard our hearts
Peacemakers	We evangelize to bring peace to the lost
Persecuted for the sake of righteousness	We endure to the end

NOTES

_____

_____

_____

_____

APPENDIX B:
FREQUENTLY ASKED QUESTIONS

Q: Which version of Scripture should I read?

A: The version isn't as important as the philosophy that was governing the translation committee. In translating Scripture, there may be more, but I believe there are three basic approaches: (1) word-for-word, (2) thought-for-thought or (3) to paraphrase.

Word-for-word is an "essentially literal" translation from the original texts ". . .taking into account differences of grammar, syntax, and idiom between current literary English and the original languages"[7] It is also known as "functional equivalence." Examples of word-for-word translations include the King James Version, the New King James Version and, most recently, the English Standard Version.

Thought-for-thought translations try to focus more on capturing the author's intent than on any literal translation of the passage. They are also referred to as the "dynamic equivalent." Unfortunately, however, it "is of necessity more inclined to reflect the interpretive opinions of the translator and the influences of contemporary culture."[8] The best known example of

---

7   Translation Philosophy, excerpted from the website for the English Standard version, http://www.esv.org/translation/philosophy
8   Translation Philosophy, excerpted from the website for the English Standard version, http://www.esv.org/translation/philosophy

a dynamically equivalent translation is the New International Version (NIV).

Finally, generally speaking, paraphrases (for example, The Living Bible, The Amplified Study Bible, etc.) are not considered legitimate translations by most scholars. While I am sympathetic to their purpose—which is to make the Word of God easier to understand, the effect tends more toward its trivialization. For this reason, I am strongly opposed to paraphrases.

Given the tendency of thought-for-thought translators to add their own interpretive bias to the text, I prefer word-for-word translations. Specifically, I use the NKJV. In fact, I will almost run when I see the NIV. I recognize that is an overreaction on my part, which will probably be shown to be due to my ignorance of the subject. For I know that many, many respected individuals and organizations use and recommend it.

Q: How do I study Scripture?

A: Hermeneutics is the science of interpretation, especially the Scripture. I am by no means a professor of hermeneutics, nor do I claim to have spent many years studying the field. Having said that, I will tell you what I have learned.[9] Generally speaking, there are countless approaches to interpreting and applying Scripture, but there seem to be at least two discernible, dominant views: the Exemplary method and the Redemptive-Historical (RH) method. Among those who hold differing views, most will affirm that God had an intended purpose for every passage of Scripture, and perhaps even for the whole of it.

Those who practice the Exemplary method see the entire Scripture as one giant book of examples from which we should

---

9   The majority of the answer to this question was learned from Professors Dan McCartney and Charles Clayton, authors of *Let the Reader Understand: A Guide to Interpreting and Applying the Bible,* and Dr. Robert Morey, author of *Studies in the Atonement.* I am indebted to these men for their work.

learn. My estimation is that this method falls short in its under-standing of the parts of Scripture in relation to the whole and tends to moralism. Consequently, those who practice and teach based on this method will often not do justice to the passage with which they are concerned. They will tend, in practice if not in theory, to present texts in a disjointed manner, and the quality or depth of their understanding and application will suffer as a result.

It's not that there aren't great examples in Scripture from which we should learn (I Corinthians 10:11-13). The question is, "Was God's primary purpose in writing Scripture to give us a book of moral lessons." To which I would answer an emphat-ic, "No." God intends so much more for His Word than we give Him or it credit for! For that reason, I personally to study and preach using the Redemptive-Historical method.

Christ inferred that the purpose of Scripture is to reveal the his-tory of redemption—from our creation and original sin, to his cross, death, and resurrection (Luke 24:13-49, note especially verse 44). Philip preached as much to the Ethiopian Eunuch (Acts 8:26-39). With this in mind, I begin by asking two ques-tions of any text: first, how does the passage point me to Christ, my Savior; and second, how shall I then live? And, by the way, I am in good company, for it seems this is exactly the method Charles Haddon Spurgeon used before it even had a name:

> From "How to Read the Bible," Charles Spurgeon, 1879 (http://www.spurgeon.org/sermons/1503.htm):   You remember the story I told you of the Welshman who heard a young man preach a very fine sermon—a grand sermon, a highfaluting, spread-eagle sermon; and when he had done, he asked the Welshman what he thought of it. The man replied that he did not think anything of it. "And why not?" "Because there was no Jesus Christ in it." "Well," said he, "but my text did not seem to run that way." "Never mind," said the Welshman, "your sermon ought to run that way." "I do not see that, however," said the young man. "No," said the other, "you do not see how

to preach yet. This is the way to preach. From every little village in England—it does not matter where it is—
there is sure to be a road to London. Though there may
not be a road to certain other places, there is certain to
be a road to London. Now, from every text in the Bible
there is a road to Jesus Christ, and the way to preach is
just to say, 'How can I get from this text to Jesus Christ?'
and then go preaching all the way along it." "Well, but,"
said the young man, "suppose I find a text that has not
got a road to Jesus Christ." "I have preached for forty
years," said the old man, "and I have never found such a
Scripture, but if I ever do find one I will go over hedge
and ditch but what I will get to him, for I will never finish without bringing in my Master . . . so that you must
not think of reading without feeling that he is there who
is Lord and Master of everything that you are reading,
and who shall make these things precious to you if you
realize him in them. If you do not find Jesus in the Scriptures, they will be of small service to you, for what did
our Lord himself say? "Ye search the Scriptures, for in
them ye think ye have eternal life, but ye will not come
unto me that ye might have life"; and therefore your
searching comes to nothing; you find no life, and remain
dead in your sins. May it not be so with us?"

With these overarching principles in mind then, following are
the general rules I try to follow when studying Scripture:

1. I pray for the knowledge and wisdom that only the Holy
   Spirit can give (James 1:5; Ephesians 1:15-22; I John
   2:27).
2. I remember that Scripture is sufficient for everything I
   need to be complete, prepared for life and godliness (2
   Timothy 3:14-17; 2 Peter 1:1-4).
3. Noting at the outset that the Bible is unlike any other
   book—in that it is the inspired, infallible, inerrant Word
   from God, I nevertheless approach the Bible like I would
   any other book. In other words, I try not to pick and

choose where I am going to study. I focus on the whole, or at the very least on a book, and then work down to the verses.

a. The Bible is a book. You wouldn't pick up a book and start in the middle of a chapter or, worse, in the middle of a sentence and try to understand its meaning. Nor should you do so with Scripture. If you've never read the Bible through from Genesis 1:1 to Revelation 22:21, START NOW! You don't need a strategy. Divide the number of pages in your Bible by 365 days. Read as many pages each day and you'll finish in a year!

    i. Note that the chapters and verses in the Bible were not a part of the original text. They are helpful for reference purposes, but they are neither inspired nor inerrant, as is the Canon of Scripture.

    ii. For that reason, I often compare the Scripture to a giant jigsaw puzzle and every verse represents a piece of the puzzle. If you've ever tried assembling a puzzle before, you know that it is extremely helpful to have at least some of the pieces around another before it is clear where a particular piece fits. I knew a professional puzzle assembler who always began assembling from the left corner of any puzzle. She would begin with one of the easier pieces to figure out and then work her way across. Others may begin from another corner, or even from the middle, and some may approach the task with no strategy whatsoever! The point—which I hope you've already understood—is that the interpretation of verses becomes clearer as you begin to see and understand more of their context.

b. You may have heard it said, "You can't see the forest for the trees," and this is frequently used in reference to someone whose focus on minutia is causing him or her to miss the big picture. Unfortunately, there are many, many churches that began or remain divided from their brothers and sisters in Christ over principles or doctrines that find their origin in one or a few verses of Scripture. Some issues are worth dividing over; most are not. When I study Scripture, I try not to get tunnel vision and allow one verse or another to become a systematic theology. I try to understand where a verse fits within the context of the forest.

c. Recalling again the overarching principle, I try to understand how a verse or passage (be they understood as puzzle pieces or trees) answers the first two questions: How does it/how do they point me to Christ? And how shall I then live?

4. If I don't understand a particular word or phrase, I try to let Scripture interpret Scripture.

5. I remember to always interpret the unclear in the light of what is clear. And, contrary to popular belief, there are statements in the Scripture that seem unclear or hard to understand (2 Peter 3:16). The problem is not with the perspicuity of Scripture, of course, but with us! For example, how are we to interpret Jesus praying to His Father in light of the doctrine of the Trinity? It is a long-held, universally embraced doctrine among Catholics and Protestants that God is One, yet Three: Father, Son, and Holy Spirit. In view of the overwhelming agreement of Scripture and church history with this doctrine, what are we to do with the few verses that seem to contradict it? The short answer is that, whatever those verses mean, they can't mean that Jesus isn't "very God of very God" because the Scripture is infallible and that would be a contradiction. So I study and pray, and pray and study until I understand or reach heaven.

6. I try to understand Scripture from a literary and grammatical standpoint.
    a. I ask myself what type of text I am reading. Is it literal? An historical narrative? Prose? Poetry or verse? Apocalyptic?
    b. Grammatically speaking, what stands out? What type of sentence is it? Is it in the imperative? Is it declarative? Inquisitive? Exclamatory?
    c. I ask: Who, what, where, when, why and how?
7. I take into consideration the historical context.
    a. When, generally, was the passage written? What about that historical period may be important to help me understand about that particular passage?
    b. Where does it fit in the history of redemption? Before the fall, after the fall, before the Law, after the Law, BC or AD?
    c. What's the cultural context? What customs do I need to understand?
8. Now, let's look at **2 Kings 6:1-6**: "And the sons of the prophets said to Elisha, 'See now, the place where we dwell with you is too small for us. Please, let us go to the Jordan, and let every man take a beam from there, and let us make there a place where we may dwell.' So he answered, 'Go.' Then one said, 'Please consent to go with your servants.' And he answered, 'I will go.' So he went with them. And when they came to the Jordan, they cut down trees. But as one was cutting down a tree, the iron ax head fell into the water; and he cried out and said, 'Alas, master! For it was borrowed.' So the man of God said, 'Where did it fall?' And he showed him the place. So he cut off a stick, and threw it in there; and he made the iron float."
    a. Believing Scripture is sufficient to help me understand and learn from such a seemingly strange and out-of-place passage, I pray for wisdom.
    b. I've read through the Bible as a whole and the passage's immediate and even relatively distant context.

c. I focus on the whole: I know this passage points to Christ and it has something to say about how I should live but, not understanding it, I start to break it down.

d. From a literary standpoint, it seems to be a historical narrative.

e. From a journalistic standpoint:

    i. "Who" is the prophet and a young trainee.

    ii. "What" they are going to make is a larger shelter in which they may live.

    iii. "Where" is on the Jordan.

    iv. "When"... not sure.

    v. "Why" is because they are out of space and the young guy is upset because his axe head fell in the river.

    vi. "How" is with the prophet's direction and manual labor.

f. Grammatically, it stands out that the young prophet makes an exclamatory statement in verse 5: "Alas, master! For it was borrowed."

g. Historically, further study reveals that the period Kings is dated corresponds with the beginning of the iron-smelting age.

h. Still, failing to understand, I ask myself a couple of questions that help me understand the significance of what I've learned:

    i. Why does the young prophet seem so upset about the axe head that sank?

        1. Letting Scripture interpret Scripture: Passages like Exodus 22 and others make it clear that anything lost while borrowed must be repaid. If the debt could not be repaid, the law of restitution required the indentured servitude of the borrower.

    ii. Why doesn't he just replace it?
1. Being the beginning of the iron-smelting age, the axe would have been extremely costly.
2. According to the law, the loss of the axe head could have resulted in an enormous debt and the young prophet's servitude, possibly for the rest of his life.

    iii. How does the passage show me my need for a savior?
1. The wages of sin is death, a debt I could never pay.
2. Just as God did for the prophet here, when He made the axe head float, Christ paid my debt on the cross.

    iv. How shall I then live?
1. Just as was true whenever a Redeemer paid a debt for another, essentially freeing the person of the obligation (as in the case of Ruth, for example), I who had the debt should now freely and willingly give myself in service to the One who paid my debt for me.

Q: Do I have to attend church?

A: Yes. God gave the church to aid and encourage growth in sanctification and to equip us for the work of the ministry. Since He gave it, attendance isn't optional. We need each other; we need the body.

"And He Himself gave some to be apostles, some prophets, some evangelists, and some pastors and teachers, for the equipping of the saints for the work of ministry, for the edifying of the body of Christ, till we all come to the unity of the faith and of the

knowledge of the Son of God, to a perfect man, to the measure
of the stature of the fullness of Christ; that we should no lon-
ger be children, tossed to and fro and carried about with every
wind of doctrine, by the trickery of men, in the cunning crafti-
ness of deceitful plotting, but, speaking the truth in love, may
grow up in all things into Him who is the head—Christ—from
whom the whole body, joined and knit together by what every
joint supplies, according to the effective working by which every
part does its share, causes growth of the body for the edifying of
itself in love." (Ephesians 4:11-16)

Q: Which church should I attend?

A: I am a Christian first, but I am also unapologetically reformed
and Presbyterian in my theology and church membership. This
is not to say that there are not Christians in every mainstream,
Christian denomination, be they of Catholic or Protestant per-
suasion. Although I have studied many of the denominations
of the Christian religion, as well as other Eastern and Western
religions, I did not base my decision to be reformed and Presbyterian on that study alone (although it was helpful). And, if
you'll remember, I was not raised in any church.

The word Presbyterian is from the Greek word *presbuteros*,
which means "elder." Presbyterian churches are called such
because they are governed by elders. Each church is governed
by elders elected by the congregation. Collectively, the elders
at a given church are referred to as the "session." At regularly
scheduled times throughout the year and as necessary, the elders from churches in the area come together to form what is
called the presbytery. Then, once a year or as needed, elders
from every church attend the general assembly. Generally
speaking, *all of the elders are considered equal (there is no hi-*
erarchy of authority) and decisions made affect the entire denomination. This stands in contrast to so many congregations
that may have fellowship together but have little in the way of
standards or consistency.

Although subordinate to the Scripture, Reformed Presbyterian churches all confess *The Westminster Confession of Faith*. Each Reformed Presbyterian denomination has minor areas of the *Confession* with which they disagree, and so they write addendums to it. After years of study, however, I have found that few (if any) other denominations preach Christ and Him crucified so passionately and consistently. If we all agreed on the basics, there would be no denominations. Yet they exist. Be assured, someone or some group, somewhere along the way, drew a line in the sand and said, "This is what we believe. We cannot, we will not, recant. So help us God!" Those lines exist for a reason. YOU must be diligent to present yourself approved—a worker who does not need to be ashamed—as one who rightly handles the Word (2 Timothy 2:15). It's as true for your church as it is for you, which is why Paul encouraged us:

"Now I plead with you, brethren, by the name of our Lord Jesus Christ, that you all speak the same thing, and that there be no divisions among you, but that you be perfectly joined together in the same mind and in the same judgment." (I Corinthians 1:10)

As I wrote earlier, for me the question was easy. I chose where I found the words of life, and Christ revealed Himself to me in the context of reformed-Presbyterian churches. The decision as to which church you attend may not be as clear-cut for you, and that's okay. As I said, I am convinced there are Christians in every mainstream Christian denomination. There are four marks of the authentic church, however, and you would do well to know and watch out for them: (1) the whole counsel of God is proclaimed; (2) the sacraments of baptism and communion are rightly celebrated; (3) church discipline is exercised; and (4) evangelism is practiced.

By speaking for "the whole counsel of God," I have in mind churches that have one emphasis or another in their teaching and rarely if ever preach or practice beyond it. That's a red flag. In an authentic church, the whole counsel—Genesis to Revelation—the history of redemption—sin and the Savior—will be faithfully proclaimed. Consistent topical preaching, bouncing from one text to another, may also be a red flag. The most faithful form of preaching is expositional, preaching from the beginning through the end of a book. In this way, the whole counsel of God is proclaimed. That's not to say that topical preaching is wrong, but if that is the regular practice of a pastor, I might consider whether I am hearing "the whole counsel of God" or just the parts that suit the preacher's agenda.

It's hard to imagine a church that doesn't practice baptism and communion, but do they observe them rightly? There is a right and wrong way to practice such, and I am not just talking about whether you sprinkle, splash, or dunk or whether the wafer is edible or tastes more like Styrofoam. Does the minister "fence the table"? Being reformed and Presbyterian, I would ask whether they baptize infants or merely dedicate them. You may be of a different opinion in this regard. Does the pastor make it clear that it is a table for believers, or is it open season on the bread and the wine? Are baptism and communion regularly observed—whether weekly, monthly, or quarterly—or is there no regularity? These are a few of the questions to ask.

Few churches today practice discipline, but the process is clearly outlined in Matthew 18:15-20 and many other passages. Before you join a church, you might ask an elder the last time the church addressed a matter of discipline. The details are irrelevant and to discuss them would be gossip, but certainly it's an appropriate question to ask in general. If he remembers a time, at least you know it happens. If he can't remember a time or somehow indicates it never happens, that's a red flag.

Finally, you can have the first three in glorious appearance, but if the church has little if any evangelistic outreach, it may just be dead. There should be some signs of missions, foreign and domestic. There should be signs of life. What is the church doing to reach the lost? What is the church doing to reach its community? If they're not doing anything, that's a red flag.

In the authentic church, all four marks will be present. A church may be stronger in one than another. Maybe that's why God led you there! But all four should be present in some form. If they're not, go find another church. It doesn't matter what the words are on the sign out in front!

Above all, remember that the church is made up of sinful men and women. Indeed, the Scripture states we all have this treasure in jars of clay (2 Corinthians 4:7-14). In other words, we are all fallible, subject to trials and temptations of every kind, but our hope is in Christ, who will one day present us all to the Father. Until then, we have the church.

Q: Do you accept speaking invitations?

A: Insofar as the Lord wills and my schedule permits, I will accept speaking engagements.

Q: How may I learn more about Hope Prison Ministries?

A: If you have Internet access, please visit our website or e-mail me at the address below. If you do not have the Internet— I will pray for you ☺.

Please contact me at:

Chandler Fozard
Hope Prison Ministries, Inc.
7600 McCart Avenue, PMB 501
Fort Worth, TX 76133
www.HopePrisonMinistries.org
chandler@HopePrisonMinistries.org

APPENDIX C:
RESOURCES AND RECOMMENDED READING

RESOURCES

PRISON MINISTRIES

HOPE PRISON MINISTRIES (the author's ministry)
7600 McCart Ave., PMB# 501
Fort Worth, TX 76133
chandler@HopePrisonMinistries.org
http://www.HopePrisonMinistries.org

REFORMED PRISON MINISTRY - a ministry of Fort Worth
Presbyterian Church (PCA)
P.O. Box 16307
Fort Worth, TX 76162
O: (817) 731-3300
F: (817) 294-5687
http://www.fortworthpca.org

MOUNT ZION BIBLE CHURCH
2603 West Wright Street
Pensacola, FLA 32505
www.MountZion.org

PRISON FELLOWSHIP
44180 Riverside Parkway
Lansdowne, VA 20176
http://www.PrisonFellowship.org

RECOMMENDED READING

Studies in The Atonement, Dr. Robert Morey, available from www.TruthDefenders.com

The Bondage of the Will, Martin Luther, translated by JI Packer and OR Johnston, available from most bookstores.

Competent to Counsel, Dr. Jay E. Adams, available from www.TimelessTexts.com and most bookstores.

More Than Redemption: A Theology for Christian Counseling, Dr. Jay E. Adams, available from www.TimelessTexts.com and most bookstores.

Don't Waste Your Life, John Piper, available from most bookstores.

Confessions by Saint Augustine.

Let the Reader Understand: A Guide to Interpreting and Applying the Bible by Professors Dan McCartney and Charles Clayton, available from most bookstores.

A Quest for More, Paul David Tripp, available from most bookstores

ACKNOWLEDGEMENTS

saved the best for last! Assuming you've just finished reading the book and you're not trying to read the end before you've read the beginning (shame on you!), you'll understand what I mean when I say I could easily fill the pages of another book with expressions of gratitude to all the people who have made this work possible. Their contributions, one and all, seem too great to prioritize. In chronological order, then, this is my list:

Thank you, first and foremost, to the God who elected me, the Son who saved me, and the Spirit who called and keeps me: my Lord and my God, blessed Three in One.

To the distant relatives who made false accusations and the state of Oklahoma, the district attorney and criminal court system of Pushmataha County in particular at the time of my sentencing, believe it or not, thank you for honoring God by being a terror to this one who did evil works! What you intended for evil—as a just sentence for my sin, God intended for good!

Thank you to Maudie and the kids for loving and forgiving me in spite of my sin.

Thank you to Pastor Dan Edwards who counseled and encouraged me with your words, letters and even provided monetary support while I was in prison.

Dear dad (my father in the faith, Michael Shelton, Mount Zion

Bible Church), thank you for sending me the Word, for bailing me out, and for your love, which covered my sin.

Dr. Robert Morey...words fail.

"Joe"—you know who you are, for teaching me that "Calvinism is much more than just what it says about salvation. . . It's a world and life view; it's a way of interpreting all of life through the lenses of Scripture."

Thank you to the Orthodox Presbyterian Church for sending me your directory and publishing my first article.

And what do you say to a man who leaves his wife and church and drives 200 hundred miles to visit you in prison regularly for just under two years? If you know, please tell Pastor Richard Shaw for me. Thank you, pastor.

Thank you to Steven Caselli, for sending me books by, among others, Jay E. Adams!

To Dr. Jay E. Adams, thank you for being supremely loving! Thank you for writing and speaking and defending the truth. I knew the gospel when I began reading your books, but you have taught me and countless others that the gospel is about more than just being pardoned from sin—it's about a life changed! Thank you also for your helpful comments and suggestions while you reviewed my manuscript. I pray this it is written "The Write Way" and that it will give many something to sink their teeth into!

To Ken, Sam, Perry and the Prison Fellowship volunteers from Asbury United Methodist in Tulsa, OK, thank you for visiting me in prison. . .and for tolerating me when I could be downright obnoxious!

Thank you to Dr. Edward Welch of CCEF for the helpful letter to my probation officer.

To Pastor Bruce Parnell, Dave and Margaret Carroll, Alan and

Liz Noell, Brad Brown and all the members of the Stillwater Reformed Presbyterian Church (Stillwater, OK), thank you for being my family and allowing me to watch in wonder at how you raised your families. At that point, you were the only godly families I had ever known!

To Rebecca and Matthew, thank you for allowing me to be a part of your lives. Rebecca, you introduced me to your best friend, who became my wife! How does one say "thank you" for something like that? Matthew, with the respect and the trust you have shown me, you have allowed me to believe that God is able to use even someone like me to help a young man like you. By God's grace, you'll be the man God intends for you to be, you'll honor Him with the gifts He's given you, and you'll live for Him all of your days! To whatever degree God has enabled me to contribute to your progress, to God be the glory!

Barbara—my love, my wife, and my joy—may I walk worthy of the treasure God has given me in you! He has appointed you to teach me how to love; and God knows, it's a full-time job! You are the sweetest, kindest, most compassionate example of God's unconditional love that I will ever witness. When I see the way you love others, I am reminded of my sin and how far I have to go. Please be patient. God isn't finished with me yet!

Dear Brandon, you're the only son I may ever know, and I wouldn't have it any other way! How many times have I wept at the grace of God in giving me a son like you; how many tears have I shed with joy when I think of the young man you're becoming? May I be the example that will encourage you to grow in grace and truth and to honor the God who saved you and brought us together!

Dear Skip, thank you for modeling for us from the pulpit what it means to preach Christ; moreover, thank you for modeling in your life what it means that to die to self is to live for Christ. Thank you also to George and Craig Chapman for your counsel and your prayers.

For being the pastor I've always wanted—the one who has no problem with me having his cell phone on speed dial to call him with all of my questions, for supporting and believing me in ways that others simply could not, for being Aquila for a day and coming along side to help me focus more clearly on why I was writing, what I was saying and how it must be said to honor God and His Word, for teaching me to appreciate the redemption I've received even more, for being an example in word and deed, thank you, Darwin Jordan. May I imitate you as you imitate Christ. I pray you'll find the rest of your congregation less troublesome!

Thank you to all the members of Fort Worth Presbyterian Church, which must be the best congregation in the PCA. It is my honor and my privilege to be a member of a congregation that so embodies the love of Christ! (Here's praying you'll still allow me to walk among you even after you've read this book.)

Thank you, especially, to Angela and Anita, who (albeit unknowingly) played a part in allowing me to reach heights in my redemption that many would have considered impossible when you asked me to teach chapel to the high-school class! In this same vein, thank you to TCA for allowing me to be a mentor to Matthew as part of your program.

Thank you to my editor, Rebecca Taff. Your initial words of encouragement surely encouraged me to press on! Thank you to Archer Ellison, aka bookcovers.com, and to all the people at LightningSource.com. This book certainly would not have come together without you!

Thank you to Woody Runner, my business partner for the last year. Thank you for modeling Christ in the way you work.

For facilitating my BSF group—when I could be at my most obnoxious—for introducing me to Woody, and for supporting me in the call, thank you to Rich.

To the men in prison to whom I have had the great honor of sharing my faith, to the men who are now reading these pages, may the God of all grace use these words concerning the comfort He has given me to comfort you, and may we all display Christ's infinite worth and supreme value in the way that we live!

And I am sure I have missed many!